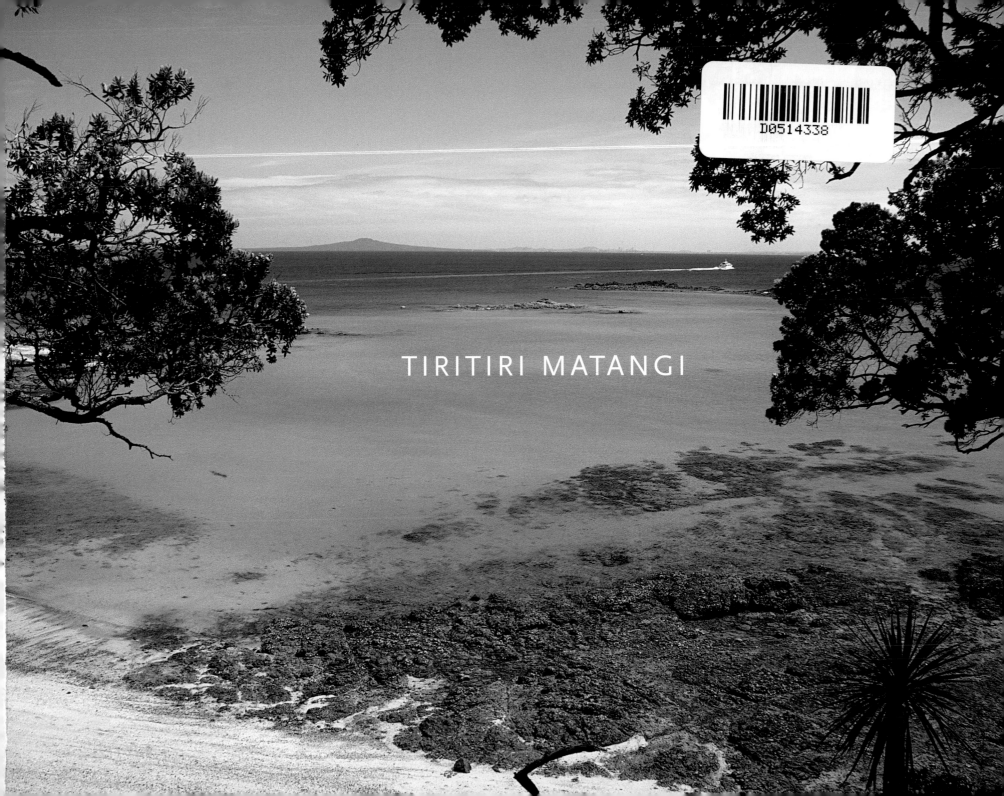

TIRITIRI MATANGI

TIRITIRI MATANGI

A MODEL OF CONSERVATION

ANNE RIMMER

TANDEM PRESS

Anne Rimmer is a member of the Supporters of Tiritiri Matangi Inc. and has been a volunteer guide on Tiri since 2000.

Educated in Wellington, she lived in Canada for 20 years, returning home in 1991. Anne lives on the North Shore of Auckland, where she has campaigned for cleaner beaches. As a Forest and Bird committee member she instigated the Millennium Forest project at the Tuff Crater just north of the Auckland Harbour Bridge.

Her wide-ranging interests include theatre, photography, travel and sailing; she is also a 'talking book' narrator for the Royal New Zealand Foundation of the Blind.

National Library of New Zealand
Cataloguing-in-Publication Data

Rimmer, Anne, 1947–
Tiritiri Matangi : a model of conservation / Anne Rimmer.
Includes bibliographical references and index.
ISBN 1-877298-16-6
1. Conservation of natural resources—New Zealand—Tiritiri
Matangi Island. 2. Tiritiri Matangi Island (N.Z.).
333.78099324—dc 22

First published in New Zealand in 2004 by
TANDEM PRESS
Auckland, New Zealand
Reprinted 2005

Design by Jacinda Torrance / Verso
Cover photo: Tiritiri Matangi from the south.
    Gareth Eyres / Exposure (courtesy of *North & South*)
Printed in China

Contents

Acknowledgements

While this book could not have been written without input from members of the Supporters of Tiritiri Matangi, the material in it is the author's own responsibility.

The knowledge, reminiscences and photographs that so many people have shared with me are now added to the archives of the island. Pat Greenfield, Wynne Spring-Rice and Annette Brown generously allowed me to use material from interviews and research they conducted some years ago.

Darcy O'Brien, Frank Arnott, Rex Mossman and Wally Sander recalled the time in the 1970s and 1980s when the Hauraki Gulf Maritime Park Board administered the island. John Craig and Neil Mitchell of the University of Auckland, who proposed the Open Sanctuary concept 20 years ago and are still involved with Tiri today, were always helpful and available. Jim Battersby, the founder of the Supporters of Tiritiri Matangi in 1988, shared memories of a subject dear to his heart, and the committee of the Supporters — especially two former chairmen, Carl Hayson and Mel Galbraith — were, aptly, 'supportive' in too many ways to recount here.

Former lighthouse keepers and family members contributed photographs and recorded their memories of an era that sadly has ended. It was a memorable experience to speak with people who had lived on Tiri before the Second World War: the King sisters (Pat Meyer, Dora Walthew and Betty Roper); Agnes Hagan, née Petty; Tiri Bourke, née Gow; and Lola Rae, née Lord, who was a sprightly 97 when I interviewed her in 2004. Similarly, for the farm history, Daisy Burrell, who also remembers Tiri pre-war, gave me access to the remarkable diaries her grandfather, E. J. Hobbs, had kept since 1893.

Paul Titchener advised on wartime activities, and former keepers Peter Taylor, Trevor Scott and Ray Walter helped with the more recent lighthouse history. I have particularly enjoyed the chance to get to know Ray and Barbara Walter better, and I thank them for their continuous encouragement and enthusiasm. They have been invaluable in recalling events of the past 20 years since the conservation project began.

Scientists and administrators from the Department of Conservation, Auckland Regional Council and universities guided me through fields I knew little about. I am grateful for their assistance. They include: Doug Arnold, Åsa Berggren, Gerry Brackenbury, Robert Brassey, Ewen Cameron, Peter Crabb, John Craig, Dave Crouchley, Shaun Dunning, Alan Esler, John Ewen, Louise Furey, Chris Gaskin, Brian Gill, Sibilla Girardet, Chris Green, Richard Griffiths, Bruce Hayward, Helen Leach, Rebecca Lewis, Tim Lovegrove, Matt Low, Rob McCallum, Sarah Macready, Don Merton, Neil Mitchell, Kevin Parker, Mike and Dee Pigneguy, Rosalie Stamp, Douglas Sutton, Jason and Shaarina Taylor, Graham Ussher, David Veart, Dick Veitch, Jan Velvin, Michael Walker, Lynda Walter and Carol West.

When I asked Graham Turbott if he would write a foreword for me, he replied that he would be honoured, but asked if it could wait till the following week, because it was his ninetieth birthday that week. There are two forewords because, when I emailed Prof. David Bellamy to tell him of the book, he replied immediately with a charmingly self-deprecating message: 'The book is a fantastic idea. This may sound big-headed but if a foreword would help, please let me know.' Similarly, Sir David Attenborough took the time to send a handwritten letter. The responses of these internationally important people compliment not me, but Tiritiri Matangi itself, and those who have made the island what it is today.

The wonderful selection of photographs has been supplied by many people, both amateur and professional (most of whom have generously donated them to the book), and the island's

Facing page: The rising sun colours the rocky eastern coast. Pat Greenfield

Page 1: The tranquil beauty of Hobbs Beach. Matt Low

Page 2: A rainbow epitomises the magic of Tiri. Matt Low

Pages 4–5: Saddlebacks, the first endangered species to be released on Tiri, in 1984, are now so numerous that Tiri birds are sent off to start new populations elsewhere. Gareth Eyres/Exposure (courtesy of *North & South*)

Tiri from the north-west. Hobbs Beach and the wharf are centre right, and the lighthouse station is top right, beyond the mown summit of Coronary Hill. The Ridge Rd and Wharf Rd are both visible. The extent of the planted areas is clear, with some striped hillsides still visible. Heletranz

archives. Photographs have come from over 50 different sources. It has been a thrill to see life restored to some of the older sepia prints through scanning and digital enhancement. Images that were so faded they would soon have disappeared altogether are now safely preserved on disk.

I am also grateful for the permission to reproduce historical images from the Auckland War Memorial Museum, Te Papa, Alexander Turnbull Library and Auckland Public Library. The Department of Conservation also lent photographs from their collection.

The Field Guide to the Birds of New Zealand, by Barrie Heather and Hugh Robertson, was my bible, to which I referred constantly.

I would like to acknowledge the part that modern technology — a fast computer, the internet and the worldwide web — have played in this project. To be able to sit at my computer at home (often at very odd hours) and exchange ideas, information and photographs with people all over the world, at great speed, is a magical experience. Even though they are such recent developments, I cannot imagine working without these modern miracles.

John Craig, Neil Mitchell, Ray and Barbara Walter, Mel Galbraith, Brian Coad, Ann Cooper, Marcel Oats and Meredith Rimmer all read drafts of the manuscript.

Cara Torrance edited the manuscript and was the project manager, and Jacinda Torrance (they are sisters) created the superb design. Helen Benton and Bob Ross at Tandem Press were kind and patient publishers, guiding a novice author through the complicated process of transforming enthusiasm and random thoughts into a coherent and beautiful publication. I am grateful for their faith in me, and for the advice and assistance of Tom Beran at Random House in the later stages of production.

I am grateful for the encouragement I received from my fellow volunteers and guides, who never failed to enquire after the book's progress when I was visiting Tiritiri Matangi. Lastly, I would like to thank my friends and my two daughters who have been so tolerant of my hermit-like behaviour, and my obsession with the subject over the past two years. Your support has been most appreciated.

Anne Rimmer
Rothesay Bay
2004

Foreword by Graham Turbott

It is perhaps not too extreme to think of Tiri as New Zealand in microcosm. As Michael King says in his *Penguin History of New Zealand*, the single-minded efforts of the settlers finally converted some 51 percent of New Zealand's surface area into grasslands — a percentage that would have been much higher but for the alpine spine of the South Island. On Tiri the process was almost complete: the island with its coastal forest and rich birdlife was quickly recognised for its good farming potential and, as described by Anne Rimmer in this fascinating story, became — except for a few minute bush remnants — just a paddock! As the author mentions, islands were, in fact, preferred by the pioneer settlers, since access by boat was so much better than struggling with ever-boggy roads.

Despite appearances sometimes to the contrary, conservation in New Zealand is at present, I believe, at a hopeful stage. Overall conservation depends, of course, upon improved land practices. But since the conservation movement began in the 1960s, the preservation of special areas, from the Save Manapouri Campaign onwards, has received widespread and enthusiastic support. Interest in predator control — a subject often viewed only with despair — has revived with the move to establish predator-free 'mainland islands', in addition to control on island sanctuaries. Often, dialogue between well-informed wildlife workers and landowners is all that is needed to work wonders for the survival of a struggling species.

The Tiri phenomenon has greatly helped the New Zealand conservation movement. The scheme proposed by John Craig and Neil Mitchell provided first for the restoration of a habitat as near as possible to the original coastal forest over the whole island, and second for unrestricted access by the public to enable all aspects of the project to be followed and publicised (the 'open sanctuary'). With sympathetic approval from the authorities, and much hard work by voluntary groups, the whole effort was an outstanding success; forest is again beginning to clothe the island, and the introduction of a number of species of endangered native birds has become possible. With the removal of the last predator, the kiore, a predator-free environment has been achieved. So much has the success of the scheme caught the public imagination that Tiri has become a symbol, throughout New Zealand, of hope for all attempting to preserve or restore our ever-dwindling remnants of native habitat.

As John Craig and Neil Mitchell clearly realised, the project — involving restoration and reintroduction — has not all been plain sailing. For example, the success of the saddleback has been astounding, whereas the kokako has encountered difficulties. All this obviously provides a useful contribution to wildlife research, helping to clarify aspects of the ecology of the species concerned.

Finally, it was quickly realised, with the beginning of the implementation of the original plan, that a resident supervisor would be essential. This would ensure that plantings remained undisturbed and no unwanted predators arrived. It would also enable visitor numbers to be tactfully controlled and would allow for those arriving to be guided. What was perhaps at first not fully realised was that Ray Walter and after 1986 his wife Barbara would, with the growth of the project, come to play this part with such distinction. When the first plantings began, Ray was still the island's lighthouse keeper — even then he took an active interest in the programme — and he and Barbara are now the key figures in this great conservation enterprise.

Graham Turbott
Auckland
June 2004

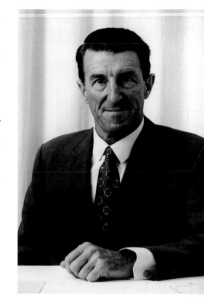

Graham Turbott in 1979.

Foreword by David Bellamy

Islands are special places. Tiritiri Matangi is very special, and, in my opinion, worthy of World Heritage status. Why? Because it is a flagship of what I like to call the 'Green Renaissance'. Clear across the world people are seeing the things and values that their parents and grandparents took for granted disappear. And instead of sitting back and letting it continue to happen they are joining forces with other like-minded souls in order to stitch their patch back into more natural working order.

Not far from Metro Auckland, Tiritiri bore the ravages of the war on the earth, stripped of its native species that made and held the soils together, its very natural history spoiled by the introduction of what became feral plants and animals. A place of sad solitude, where real people came to face an ever-bleaker future, a sameness creeping across the world.

Just as the Galapagos and the islands of the Malaysian archipelago inspired Charles Darwin and Alfred Russell Wallace to write that first paper on evolution by natural selection (a scientific paper that changed the way humankind thought about itself), so Tiritiri inspired an ever-growing bank of people from all walks of life to challenge the fitness of their species in the struggle for future survival.

One of the most inspiring days I ever spent was working with a group of children planting native species back on that multicoloured and pleasant land for Peter Hayden's television series, 'Moa's Ark'. My proudest moment was meeting a takahe chick called Bellamy enjoying its island home.

Please read this book, then go see the island for yourselves. But when you do, be careful where you tread. Take home only the song of native birds and the resolve to become an active part of the Green Renaissance that is putting the humaneness of natural history back into the world.

David Bellamy
Bedburn
June 2004

David Bellamy on Tiri, December 1998.
Mel Galbraith

Above left: Tiritiri Matangi – an island worthy of World Heritage status.
Gareth Eyres / Exposure (courtesy of *North & South*)

Facing page: In safe hands: research done on Tiri helps conservation throughout New Zealand. This stitchbird chick has a brighter future.
Pat Greenfield

Map labels:
Marsden Point
Bream Head
Lady Alice
Mauitaha
Coppermine
Whatupuke
Hen and Chickens Group
Bream Bay
Taranga
Sail Rock
Waipu Cove
Bream Tail
McGregor Rock
Mangawhai Heads
Sentinel Rock
Te Arai Point
Pakiri
Goat
Leigh
Warkworth
Tawharanui Marine Park
Kawau
Mahurangi
Beehive
Moturekareka
Motutara
Motuora
Saddle (Te Haupa)
Wenderholm Reserve
Orewa
Tiritiri Matangi
Whangaparaoa
Long Bay Marine Reserve
Rakino
Motutapu
Rangitoto
Motuihe
Browns
Waiheke
Pakatoa
Rotoroa
Ponui
Auckland
Waitemata Harbour
Manukau Harbour
Hunua Ranges
Miranda

Mokohinau (Pokohinu)
Groper Rock
Burgess
Trig (Atihau)
Hokoromea (Flax)
Fanal
N
Rakitu
Little Barrier (Hauturu)
Kaikoura
Great Barrier (Aotea)
Hauraki Gulf
Channel
Cape Colville
Port Jackson
Cuvier
Colville Bay
Great Mercury
Whangapoua
Motukawao Group
Coromandel
Cow and Calf
Te Kouma Harbour
Whitianga
Manaia
Kirita Bay
Coromandel Peninsula
Firth of Thames
Thames
Whangamata

0   10   20   30   40 km

Map reproduced courtesy of Linda Bercusson. From *The Hauraki Gulf: from Bream Head to Cape Colville.*

About this book

This book is written for the general reader, but aims to include all the essential scientific and historical facts about the island. The chapters are organised roughly chronologically and by subject.

The island is referred to as 'Tiri' throughout, and many of the players are referred to by their first names, which is common practice in the 'classless' New Zealand society.

The book is not intended as a field guide to birds or plants, giving instead only those facts that are relevant in the Tiri context. In general, only the common names of flora and fauna are used in the text, with scientific names of the main organisms being given in the appendices. The appendices cover the birds, the trees and plants, the lighthouse keepers and signalmen, the chairs of the Supporters, the major sponsors and the key people.

Unless otherwise noted, all photographs were taken on Tiri. The photographer's name appears alongside each photograph.

References given as 'B1, B53' etc. in the notes section refer to the quarterly bulletin of the Supporters of Tiritiri Matangi. Since 2001 this bulletin has been known as the *Dawn Chorus*.

Supporters of Tiritiri Matangi Inc.
PO Box 90 814
Auckland Mail Centre
Auckland, New Zealand
Telephone (Tiritiri Matangi Island): +64 9 476 0010
Website: www.tiritirimatangi.org.nz

Annual subscription (2004):
Single adult, family, or corporate $20
Overseas $25
Student, child $5

New Zealand birdsong can be heard at the website of Kiwi Wildlife Tours: www.kiwi-wildlife.co.nz

Introduction

This book tells the story of one small island, and of the people for whom the word 'Tiri' has a special resonance.

From my home, on Auckland's North Shore, I can see Tiritiri Matangi floating on the horizon. The lovely sight has been my constant inspiration over the two-year gestation of this book. I am a scientist, by training and inclination. Before I started my research, I knew I would enjoy the ecological side of it, but I wasn't so sure about all that history. However, alongside the pleasure of learning more about the flora and fauna, I quickly became obsessed with gleaning more facts about a person or a long-vanished building, rejoicing when a photograph or an old newspaper cutting enabled me to fit another piece into the jigsaw puzzle. It has been a most enjoyable journey, made more so by the interesting people I have met along the way.

My own involvement with Tiri is comparatively recent. I first visited with my daughters, soon after returning from Canada in 1991. My experiences during my 20-year 'OE' had made me anxious to become involved in keeping my homeland as clean, green and unspoiled as possible.[1] A working weekend on Tiri with the North Shore branch of Forest and Bird whetted my appetite for a deeper involvement with the Supporters, and I was an early recruit when the formal guiding programme started in 1998.

Visiting on a regular basis — I try to guide at least fortnightly — allows me to follow the flow of the seasons, and chart the changes on the island. I can appreciate the growth of the trees and the noticeable increase in the numbers of birds, especially over the past few years. And I can monitor the ups and downs of the precious takahe and kokako families. I get great satisfaction from having suggested the names for two takahe chicks, Kristina and Blake, and it is pure joy to experience close-up encounters with the kokako, Te Koha Waiata, whose lovely name means 'The Gift of Song'.

Many schools visit Tiri. This group is entering Little Wattle Valley near the end of their guided tour.
Gareth Eyres / Exposure (courtesy of *North & South*)

Tiritiri Matangi is an island that is doubly blessed: firstly, because it carries that most romantic and enduring of man-made structures, a lighthouse; and secondly, because, largely through the work of volunteers, it has been transformed into a remarkable wildlife sanctuary — one that is open to the public. It is a joyous place that never fails to touch people. Over 33,000 visitors experience the island's magic each year.

For 140 years the Tiritiri light has symbolised a safe haven and security for mariners. Now, the island provides an equally

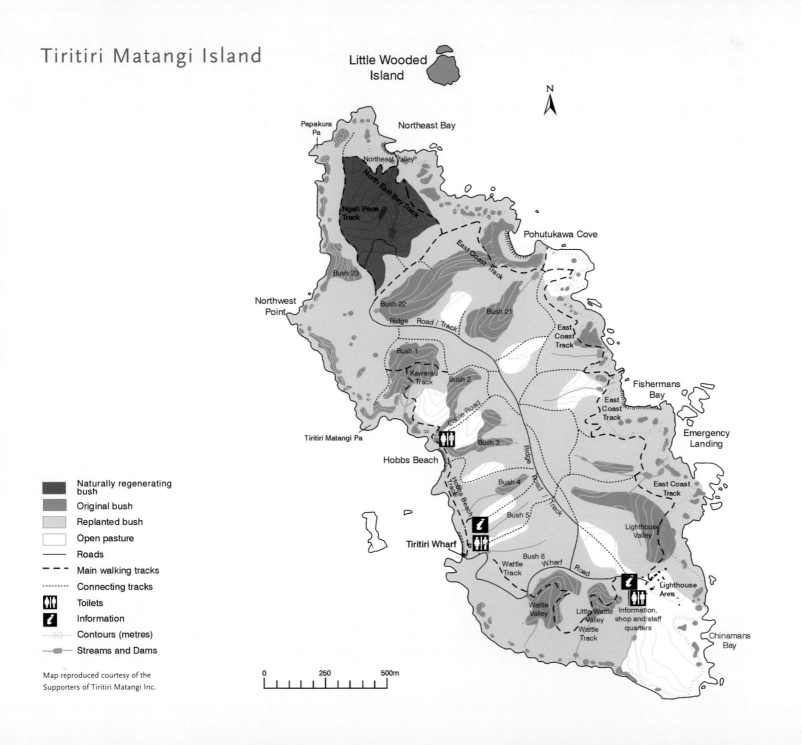

Tiritiri Matangi Island

Little Wooded Island

N

Papakura Pa

Northeast Bay

Northeast Valley

North East Bay Track

Ngati Paoa Track

Pohutukawa Cove

Bush 23

East Coast Track

Northwest Point

Bush 22

Bush 21

Ridge Road / Track

East Coast Track

Bush 1

Kawerau Track

Bush 2

East Coast Track

Fishermans Bay

Cable Road

Bush 3

Emergency Landing

Tiritiri Matangi Pa

Hobbs Beach

Ridge Road / Track

Bush 4

East Coast Track

Hobbs Beach Track

Bush 5

Tiritiri Wharf

Lighthouse Valley

Bush 6

Wattle Track

Wharf Road

Wattle Valley

Little Wattle Valley

Lighthouse Area

Wattle Track

Information, shop and staff quarters

Chinamans Bay

Legend

- Naturally regenerating bush
- Original bush
- Replanted bush
- Open pasture
- Roads
- Main walking tracks
- Connecting tracks
- Toilets
- Information
- 30 — Contours (metres)
- Streams and Dams

0   250   500m

safe haven for New Zealand's endangered wildlife.

The story's beginnings are shrouded in the mists of time before humans reached New Zealand. The Maori inhabitation of Tiritiri Matangi, which ended abruptly in the early nineteenth century, was followed by a period of farming that rendered the island as barren as the New Zealand mainland. Alongside this runs the convoluted history of the lighthouse and those that cared for it. The story culminates in the germination, growth and fruition of the remarkable process that produced the Tiritiri Matangi Island Open Sanctuary, which today is a conservation success story of international significance.

Over 10 years, from 1984 to 1994, thousands of volunteers planted over 280,000 trees on Tiri. In place of bare farmland, the island is now clothed in a flourishing young forest that rings with birdsong. As a result of this remarkable effort, thousands of New Zealanders feel they have a stake in this Open Sanctuary. Twelve species of threatened or endangered fauna have been introduced to the predator-free island, where they thrive so well that the island's surplus birds are sent to seed new populations elsewhere.

The island is now administered and staffed in a partnership between the Department of Conservation and the Supporters of Tiritiri Matangi Inc., a non-governmental organisation.

Since the island is still very much a 'work in progress', this book presents a snapshot, recording Tiritiri Matangi as it is at the start of the new millennium. In fact, one could say that change is the only constant on Tiri. Certainly, as the book's publication date loomed, I found myself checking the island from my windows each morning, fearful lest someone had decided to paint the lighthouse red again!

The takahe, JJ, patrols her patch around the historic lighthouse.
Gareth Eyres/Exposure
(courtesy of *North & South*)

Timeline

c.1400   Maori first visit Tiri

c.1500   Maori living on the island. Kiore introduced

1821   Maori inhabitants driven off by muskets

1841   New Zealand Government assumes ownership of Tiri as a lighthouse reserve

1864   Lighthouse and two keepers' cottages built

1865   Lighthouse first illuminated 1 January 1865, burning colza (canola) oil

1879   Lighthouse converted to paraffin oil

1898   Telegraphic line to Waiwera. 'Morse House' built

   E. J. (Johnny) Hobbs helping on Tiri

1902   Hobbs has Tiri farm lease

1906–09   Keeper is Anders Hansen

c.1911   Big fire destroys much of the bush

1912   Signal Station built/modified for Auckland Harbour Board (AHB), two signalmen and two keepers in residence

   Chief Signalman's (Principal Keeper's) house built

   'The Fourth House' from Greys Ave brought to the island

1914–18   First World War

1916   Light converted to incandescent kerosene burner 22 February 1916

1918   Two new keepers' houses built

   Slaughter's Gun Cotton Fog Signal

c.1922   Big fire

1925   Lighthouse automated. Flashing acetylene light 30 April 1925

   Island under AHB administration — three signalmen. Keepers withdrawn

1928   King and Davies families arrive on Tiri

1935   Diaphonic foghorn installed

   Radio beacon (navigation aid) installed

1939–45   Second World War

1939   Royal Naval Reservists arrive

1940   Port War Signal Station (PWSS) built near lighthouse

   Hobbs removes his stock

1941   Army Fortress Observation Post (FOP) built

1942   PWSS building moved to centre of island

1945   AHB returns after war (three signalmen)

1946   Hobbs' stock returned

1947   AHB closes signal station 1 July 1947

   Lighthouse keepers return. Tower painted white

1950s   Workshop and engine shed built

1954–
c.1970   Fred Ladd and Bruce Packer, Tourist Air Travel Ltd, flew the skies over Tiri

1955   Diesel generator installed. Electricity powers the light

c.1955   Principal Keeper's house demolished

1957   Radio beacon deactivated

1962   Lenses on lighthouse adjusted, making existing light brighter

1965   Relieving keepers' quarters ('The Bach') built

   Davis Marine Light (11 million candlepower) first illuminated 12 March 1965

1967   Underwater cable from Whangaparaoa. Mains power

   Hauraki Gulf Maritime Park (HGMP) formed

1970   142 hectares of Tiri designated Recreation Reserve

1970
& 1971   Alan Esler, DSIR botanist, visits

1971   Hobbs' farm lease not renewed. Tiri to be left for bush to regenerate

1974   Kakariki release in January

   John Craig first visits Tiri in February

   Auckland University accommodation in woolshed, Hobbs Beach

1975   Remaining 64 hectares included in Recreation Reserve

   Lighthouse staff reduced to one keeper

1978	Neil Mitchell's first visit
	Woolshed demolished
	University puts prefab accommodation in Bush 3
1980	Island is Tiritiri Matangi Island Scientific Reserve within HGMP
	Keeper Ray Walter arrives
1982	Visit of Sir Peter Scott, World Wildlife Fund
	Management Plan for Tiri
1983	Revegetation Manager Michael Cole arrives
	First meeting of Tiri committee of HGMP Board, held on Tiri, 20 July 1983
	Nursery complex built
	First test plots of 1200 pohutukawa planted
1984	Saddleback release (22 from Cuvier) 25 February 1984
	Mike Cole leaves
	Light automated with quartz iodine light (1.6 million cp)
	Last keeper (Ray Walter) withdrawn
	Electronic foghorn installed
	Bunkhouse set up in lower house
1984–94	Planting period. 30,000 trees per year = 280,000 trees
1985	University hut removed from Bush 3
1986	Ray Walter becomes permanent Lands and Survey employee
1987	DOC established, absorbing HGMP Board
	Six brown teals released
1988	Supporters of Tiritiri Matangi Inc. formed in October
1989	Mains power is lost when cable fails for third time; light reverts to diesel generator
	Wattle Track completed
	First public release of 40 whiteheads on 3 September 1989 (40 more on 29 May 1990)
1990	Lighthouse solar-powered, automated and de-manned
	Second release of brown teals 8 July 1990
	HGMP Board abolished 17 July 1990
1990	Penguin viewing boxes built

1991	Takahe release (two birds, Mr Blue and Stormy) 26 May 1991
	New generator installed July 1991. Power is part solar, part diesel. Light is 300,000 cp
1992	Visit of Duke of Edinburgh, WWF, 1 March 1992
	First takahe chick, Matangi (F) hatches (egg from Maud Island)
	Forty-four North Island robins (from pine plantation near Rotorua) released 12 April 1992
1993	Takahe, Matangi, dies at 10 months
	Five pairs of little spotted kiwi released 4 July 1993
	Poison drop eradicates kiore rats, 29 September 1993
	Bellbird breeding on Whangaparaoa, December 1993
1994	Kawerau Track opened
	Last planting ceremony. Total trees planted since 1994 = 283,000
1995	Lighthouse closed to public 4 May 1995
	Thirty-seven stitchbirds (from Little Barrier Island) released 3 September 1995
1996	Takahe, Mr Blue, died 26 November 1996
1997	Three kokako released 10 August 1997
1998	New wharf built
	Four more kokako released 21 March 1998
	Supporters win Loder Cup
	Supporters' tenth anniversary
1999	First guides' meeting 26 June 1999
2000	Tiri wins inaugural ARC Environmental Award
	Argentine ants discovered
	Kakariki breeding at Whangaparaoa
2001	Thirteen fernbirds released throughout June
	Implement sheds completed
2002	Lighthouse boosted to 1.2 million cp
2003	Wharf shelter built
	Sixty tuatara (from Middle Island) released 25 October 2003
2004	Thirty-two tomtits (from Hunuas) released 14 April 2004

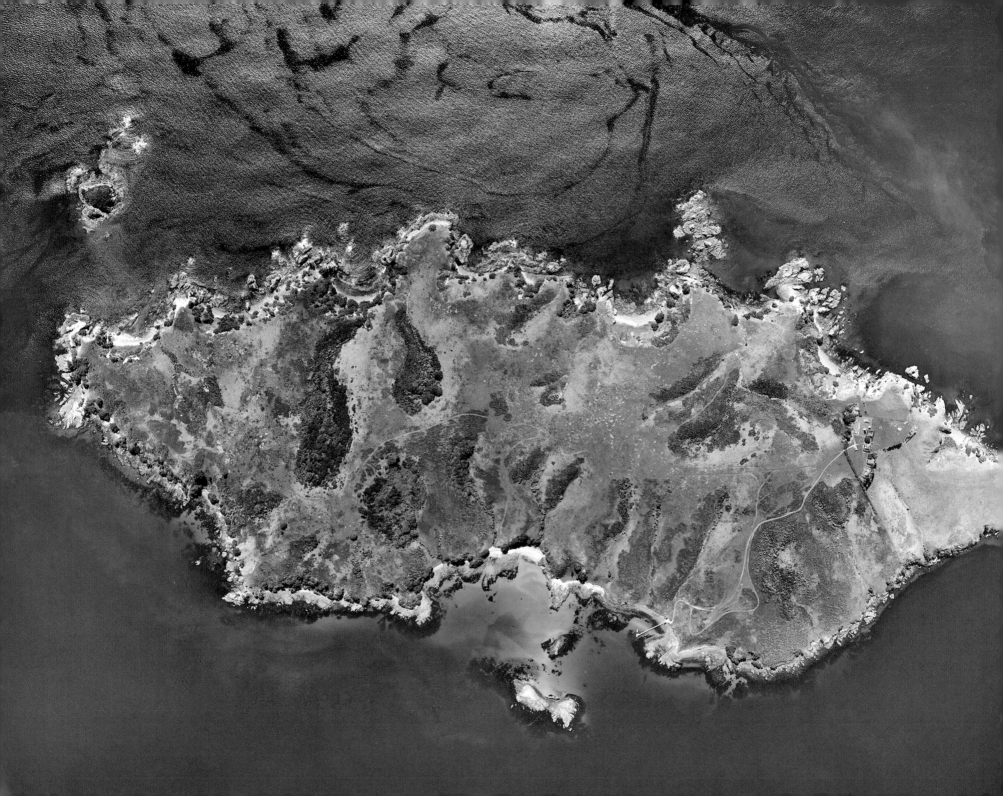

ONE

NOW — AND THEN

Tiritiri Matangi Island lies in the centre of the Hauraki Gulf, four kilometres off the Whangaparaoa Peninsula, which has Shakespear Regional Park at its tip. To the west is North Shore City, one of New Zealand's fastest-growing and most affluent regions, whose cliffs and beaches are lined with houses. The city of Auckland, with one million people, lies 28 kilometres (16 nautical miles) to the south. Huge container ships pass close to Tiri and the sea is often dotted with pleasure craft.

The Hauraki Gulf is a sheltered body of water, surrounded by land on three sides, with Great Barrier and Little Barrier Islands protecting the exposed north-eastern side.

Tiri is a small island, about three kilometres long and less than one kilometre wide, covering approximately 220 hectares. Its long axis lies north-west to south-east. The exposed 'east' coast (as it is generally known), with its sheer cliffs and rocky coastline, is more rugged than the sheltered 'west' coast, which faces the mainland and has the only sandy beach.

From much of the mainland, the long, low silhouette of Tiri resembles a sleeping hippopotamus. The highest point is the 'trig' near the centre of the island at about 90 metres altitude, while the lighthouse, at the southern end, stands at about 70 metres.

During the last period of ice ages, some 70,000–14,000 years ago when the sea level was 50–130 metres lower than at present, Tiri (like the other Gulf islands) was merely a tree-clad hill in the vast Hauraki Plain. As the world warmed and the ice retreated during the Holocene era, the sea level rose, flooding the Hauraki Gulf and isolating Tiri.[1]

The island is composed of old, hard, dark rocks, part of the 'Greywacke Basement', formed while New Zealand was still part of Gondwanaland.[2] The dark greywacke contrasts with the pale, easily eroded cliffs of Waitemata sandstone and mudstone on the mainland opposite. On Tiri this younger layer — all 1.5 kilometres of it — has eroded down to the bedrock, except for a small area at the north of the island.

Greywacke also forms Kawau Island and Tawharanui Peninsula to the north of Tiri, and Motutapu and Waiheke Islands to the south, continuing on to the Hunua Ranges on the mainland.[3]

Rangitoto Island lies to the south, its lava flows almost joining it to the much older Motutapu Island. This very young shield volcano erupted out of the sea only 600 years ago.

The name Tiritiri Matangi, which translates as 'buffeted by the wind', says it all: it is a rare day when a wind is not blowing on Tiri. Usually it blows harder there than anywhere else. The highest gusts recorded were over the 90-knot maximum on the measuring apparatus.

The sculpted trees on the eastern cliffs attest to the wind's force, while those on the sheltered western side have a more upright form. High winds carry salt spray right across the island, burning the leaves. Strong winds can topple trees in the forest, opening up light wells where seedlings spring up. Summer winds are especially hard on plants, drying them out, and baking the soil until great cracks appear in the clay at the top of the island.

Tiri is naturally a dry island. The islands of the Hauraki Gulf

Facing page: Aerial view of Tiritiri Matangi, c.1980, before planting started, showing forest remnants in the gullies. The brown areas are bracken. A road leads from the lighthouse station, far right, down to the wharf. The university hut can just be seen in the Y-shaped gully at centre.
Tiri Archives

On the East Coast Track, looking north to Kawau Island. Margaret Chappell

In fine weather the island sparkles, the sea sapphire-blue and glittering, and the shiny coats on the leaves of many plants are like tiny mirrors reflecting the sun. The still days of winter are rare and magical: a smooth, silvery sea blends seamlessly into a grey sky, and not a breath of wind stirs the leaves.

have drier climates than the adjacent mainland because the region's weather comes from the west. Clouds, rising to cross the Waitakere Ranges, drop their rain on Auckland, so that by the time they reach Tiri the clouds have no more rain. Often it can be pouring in Auckland, while the sun shines on Tiri.

Annual rainfall is low, about 750–1100 millimetres, and most of the small streams on the island dry out in summer. The only natural spring is in Lighthouse Valley, and the seven ponds are all at man-made dams constructed during the reafforestation period. The recently completed wetlands in the Northeast Valley contain the largest bodies of water on the island, with 1000 and 875 square metres behind the two dams.

The island's climate is equable, its temperatures being moderated by the surrounding sea. In summer the highs are about 20–25 degrees Celsius, a little lower than on the mainland,

but conversely the winter temperature seldom falls below seven degrees Celsius, which is higher than on the mainland. Frosts are rarely recorded.

In Maori legend it is a sign of settled weather if Tiri appears to float above the horizon.

Tiritiri Matangi was originally covered in rich forest. A raucous multitude of seabirds nested within the forest in burrows, which they shared with tuatara. Their droppings left rich deposits of guano, which resulted in an extremely fertile soil on the island. Gulls, terns and shags nested on the rocks.

Many land birds were also present and Tiri's primeval forest would have rung with birdsong: bellbird choirs, tui mimicry, the tremulous music of the grey warbler, the feathery whistle of the kereru's wings, the distinctive calls of the kaka by day and the morepork and kiwi by night.

~

TWO

A TIME OF PLENTY — THE MAORI

Then came the Maori, master navigators who may have found Aotearoa in part by following whales and migratory birds such as long-tailed cuckoos, muttonbirds and shorebirds.

The arrival of humans wrought great change upon New Zealand as a whole, from which Tiri's island status did not spare it.

The Auckland region, rich in natural resources, was settled about 800 years ago, and for these natural seafarers, with their powerful waka and their reliance on seafood, the Gulf islands were an important part of their domain.

Although it is not known exactly when Tiri was first inhabited, Maori were certainly living on neighbouring Motutapu Island before Rangitoto erupted; in the ash layers left by the eruptions are the footprints of people, both adults and children, and of dogs.[1]

Imagine the surprise of the people living in the Hauraki Gulf when the sea began to boil, and a whole new island appeared. Even though these Pacific travellers would have known of volcanoes from their homeland, the sight of a fiery island rising out of the sea and the night-long pyrotechnics must have been both wondrous and terrifying.

By the time of the Rangitoto eruptions, Maori were using Tiritiri Matangi as a temporary campsite and hunting and fishing base. They caught mainly large prey such as marine mammals, including sea lions and bottle-nosed dolphins, and fish such as sharks, rays and snapper. They ate tuatara. They also caught many coastal and bush birds, including the king shag, which is now very rare. Shellfish made up a very small proportion of the Maori diet. Clearly, there was abundant protein food available at this time.

Bracken fern was an important food source to Maori because it was available year-round. Some of the forest on Tiri was burned soon after human arrival, possibly deliberately to establish gardens or to encourage the growth of bracken fern. The starchy roots of the bracken were 'roasted over embers, beaten open and then chewed laboriously — a process that caused great tooth-wear'.[2]

Polynesian explorers took with them a standard set of food plants, including taro, coconuts, bananas, kumara, yams and

Tiri from afar.
Matt Low

In Maori tradition Tiritiri Matangi Island is one of the floats of an ancestral fishing net.[3]

breadfruit to plant in new lands; but, being tropical in origin, many of these plants could not grow in New Zealand's colder climate.[4] When Maori planted gardens in Tiri's fertile soil, their tropical crops would have fared better in the island's milder winter temperatures than they did on the mainland.

Nevertheless, some crops could no longer be grown year-round as in tropical Polynesia, and methods of storage had to be devised to protect root crops such as kumara over the cold winter months.[5] Kumara pits can still be seen as shallow rectangular hollows in specially mown areas on Tiri.

Archaeology

What we know of the early Maori presence on Tiri comes from archaeological surveys, investigation of the wharf site, Maori Land Court records and anecdotal evidence from Maori.

In 1981, Wynne Spring-Rice, an archaeology graduate student at Auckland University, recorded 26 sites such as dwelling terraces, middens (rubbish dumps) and kumara pits.

Then, in 1996–97, erosion from two cyclones uncovered some settlement evidence in a bank near the wharf. DOC archaeologists excavated a small portion of this site before it was covered by the new wharf construction. They found three layers of habitation from about 1400–1500 AD, which are very early settlement dates for the Auckland region.

Archaeological sites are protected under the provisions of the Historic Places Act (now updated to 1993). Wynne Spring-Rice made sure that Tiri's archaeological sites were protected during the planting period, though this sometimes brought her into conflict with those who were more interested in planting trees or protecting birds. For example, excavation for a toilet was halted when a midden was revealed — the layers of shells can still be seen at the southern end of Hobbs Beach.

As far as is known, moa did not live on Tiri. (They were rapidly becoming scarce on the mainland by the early fifteenth century.) Moa bone, which is solid and dense, was useful for making tools and fish-hooks. One bone from a small moa has been found in a Tiri midden but it appears to have been brought to the island, most likely as part of a meal.

The Maori kept dogs as pets and for hunting, but also as a source of food. They were fed food scraps and fish in times of plenty, but were killed and eaten if food was short. The dog skins were used for clothing, for example, for decorating cloaks.[6] A large number of dog remains have been found during excavations on Tiri.

Stone tools such as adzes took a great effort to make, and the best materials were sought out for them. Greywacke, which is found on several islands of the Gulf, including Tiri, was flaked into adzes and other tools. Other stone materials, including basalt and obsidian, were brought in from the Coromandel area and Mayor Island (Tuhua) in the Bay of Plenty. The green-coloured obsidian found on Mayor Island was highly prized for making smaller tools for cutting and skinning, and flakes of this obsidian have been found on Tiri.

The Polynesian rat, kiore (*Rattus exulans*), was brought to Tiri by the Maori. Polynesians took kiore with them in their canoes, releasing them on islands throughout the Pacific as a future food source. This is why Maori regard kiore as taonga (treasure) rather than as the vermin that Pakeha consider rats to be. It is similar to Europeans leaving goats on remote islands as 'castaway supplies'.

The introduction of kiore will undoubtedly have affected Tiri's original flora and fauna — the only land mammals in New Zealand before then were bats (see Chapter 12, 'The Unwanted'). Though kiore are primarily vegetarians, they also eat insects and can climb trees to reach birds' eggs and young.

Maori probably began living permanently on Tiri during the fifteenth century. They built houses and made a stone retaining wall near the beach. It may have been an eruption of Rangitoto that caused a tsunami during this period. The wave carried a layer of fine beach gravel inland well above the usual sea level, and would have inundated settlements near the beach.

The earliest inhabitants of Tiri had lived in undefended settlements near the sea. Then, during the sixteenth century, as tribal warfare increased, two pa were built on easily defended sites.

Tiritiri Matangi Pa, after which the island is named, was built by the Kawerau tribe on a headland north of Hobbs Beach. This is a spectacular site above sheer cliffs looking west towards Whangaparaoa (Bay of Whales) and south as far as Rangitoto and Motutapu. The pa on the volcanoes of the Auckland isthmus were visible in the distance, and any approaching waka would have been easily seen.

The smaller Papakura Pa (Red Rocks) was established by the Ngati Paoa tribe at the northern tip of the island. This pa was destroyed in the 1700s during fighting between the two tribes.

Each pa probably had fewer than 50 people living in it. The pa dwellers planted their gardens within the forest to conceal them from raiders. One such garden was located at the top of Bush 22. Kumara and gourds may have been grown there.

In 1821 the Ngapuhi tribe under Hongi Hika swept south through the Hauraki Gulf. Armed with muskets, they massacred

Differing opinions

Of all the academic disciplines one might expect that archaeology would have facts that were 'set in stone'. However, there is lively debate on some subjects, for example the carcinogenicity of bracken fern. Douglas Sutton believes that bracken is carcinogenic, causing stomach cancer; Louise Furey says it is not; while others, such as Helen Leach, question which part of the plant is implicated, or whether the method of preparation used by the Maori may have reduced or eliminated the effect. In any case, most early Maori would have died young before they could succumb to cancer.[7]

Motutapu and Rangitoto Islands from Tiri.
Anne Rimmer

the Kawerau people. The survivors fled, many going south to the Waikato to join related tribes. The Church Missionary Record of 1833 recorded that the whole coast was desolate and without inhabitants.[8] Tiri, like the rest of the region, was left deserted.

In 1841, in the absence of the Kawerau people, the Ngati Paoa sold the entire 'Mahurangi Block' (which extended from Te Arai, near Mangawhai, to Takapuna) to the Crown. Interestingly, Tiri does not appear on the map in the deed of sale. Small groups of Kawerau people slowly returned to their ancestral lands, but not in any numbers to Tiri.

In later periods, groups of Maori made seasonal visits to Tiri to fish for sharks and gather fern root. The coastline between Whangaparaoa and Matakana provided a highly valued seasonal resource: the *muru* or small spotted shark, which could be caught and dried as a winter food source.

In a Native Land Court hearing of 1867, Matini Murupaenga and others made a claim on Tiri, stating in part that their ancestors 'lived there and cultivated there, were buried there and had built a pa there'. However, Judge Fenton decided that Tiritiri Matangi, which by this date was a lighthouse reserve, should remain in the Crown's possession.

A kiore. John Craig

The naming of things

As with the history of the island there are various opinions on the translation of the Maori name for the island, Tiritiri Matangi, although it is generally translated as 'wind blowing about', or 'buffeted by the wind'. Some alternative translations are:

Tiritiri-o-matangi is 'the sanctified heaven of fragrant breezes'.[9]

'Tiritiri is a twig placed in the ground to indicate the position of a kumara tuber, matangi, the warm north-east breeze.'[10]

'The gathering place of the winds on the north-east horizon where the kumara grow.'

The first written record of Tiritiri Matangi appears to be in 1821, by Captain James Downie, commander of HMS *Coromandel*, which anchored at Waiwera on 19 May 1821 after sailing north through the Tiri Channel. Downie marked 'Teere Teere Matangi' on his chart.[11] Dumont d'Urville, who sailed south through the Tiri Channel on *Astrolabe* on 24 February 1827, recorded the island as 'Tiri-Tiri-Matangui'.[12]

The two pa sites, Tiritiri Matangi and Papakura, were named by their Maori inhabitants. Some of the geographical names, such as Hobbs Beach and Chinamans Bay, relate to early farming or lighthouse activities.

The botanist, Alan Esler, named some of the natural features in his 1971 report to the Hauraki Gulf Maritime Park Board, for example, Northeast Bay and Pa Point. He named the streams, for example, Puriri Creek and Pohutukawa Creek. However, these stream names are little used today.

The *Søren Larsen* sailing off Hobbs Beach. Anne Rimmer

The areas of mature bush in the valleys were numbered by the University of Auckland researchers in the mid-1970s. For example, the Kawerau Track runs through Bush 1 and 2, and the university hut was in Bush 3. Regrettably, these prosaic labels remain the only identification for the forested areas.

Other names are more recent; for example, Kawerau Track, Blackmore's Seat, and a few vernacular names such as Coronary Hill and Graham's Road have come into common usage. Stretches of the boardwalks and tracks are generally identified as being near a particular feeder, water trough or seat.

Above: Pohutukawa at Northeast Bay. Miriam Beatson

THREE

THE PASTORAL CENTURY

Why would anyone choose to farm on an island, especially at a time when the mainland of New Zealand was barely settled? In the early days of the colony, particularly in 'the roadless north', most transport was by water, making an island just as accessible as anywhere else on the coast.[1] In fact, islands were favoured because they required no fences, thus saving costs.

Tiritiri Matangi Island had additional advantages: a warmer climate than the mainland, very fertile soil, and land that had been partially cleared by the Maori. Tiri was Crown land, and a lighthouse reserve from 1841, with the majority of the island being leased for farming.

The Native Land Court for Tiritirimatangi [sic] 1867, recorded that 'Messrs Taylor, MacMillan and Campbell, lived on the island at a very early date', and Captain Thomas Duder 'occupied the island' with his six sons from 1860–66. 'I had a house there,' Duder told the Court. 'I had sheep. … I bought the pig of Duncan Campbell who was living there before me.' There is no record of where Campbell or Duder lived, but later farm buildings were located at Hobbs Beach. Joseph Schollum was farming there about 1896, and a Mr Dennis succeeded him.[2]

When Everard John (Johnny) Hobbs of Whangaparaoa took over the Tiri lease in 1902 he had already worked on the island for previous leaseholders, including the Shakespear family, who also farmed Little Barrier Island from 1897. Hobbs, who had taught himself to read and write, kept diaries from 1890 to the 1930s of which many survive. His daily entries record the weather, and detail his work as a farm labourer, drover, shearer, gum digger and farmer. He worked almost every day, and seems to have travelled huge distances. For example, in November 1899:

2 November Thur: I got up early and went up to town by the Kotiti. W. fine.

3 November Fri: In town and went down to Tiri Tiri by the Kapanui and got the sheep in and started to clean them in the afternoon. W. squally.

4 November Sat: At Tiri all day getting the sheep in and cleaning them in the afternoon. W squally. Blowing hard from West.

5 November Sun: Over at Tiri. W. fine.

6 November Mon: Over at Tiri. A light shower or two.

7 November Tues: Came home from Tiri in the morning.[3]

Everard John Hobbs.
Daisy Burrell

As well as using the steamer services, Hobbs sailed in the Shakespears' yacht, but on other occasions he rowed across to Tiri from Whangaparaoa and worked a day or two, sometimes having to wait for the weather to improve before he could row home again.

The farm on Tiri covered 200 hectares (though much of this was in bush) while the remaining 20 hectares was the lighthouse reserve at the southern end. It was rough pasturing on danthonia, a native grass, but after some burning off and planting of pasture grasses, Hobbs was running 672 sheep on the island by 1905.[4] At the same time, he was farming on Whangaparaoa.

The Crown Lands ranger, J. D. Steedman, recorded in 1908 that 'About 400 acres [98 ha] are in grass, and the balance ... scrub bush, few cabbage trees, & few Birch [mapou]'. Steedman felt that the manuka could be cut for fuel, but he was emphatic that 'This suggestion does not apply to Pohutukawa trees which should be rigidly conserved.' Thus we have an early ranger to thank for the preservation of the magnificent old pohutukawa that fringe Tiri's cliffs.

Hobbs' 1905 diary records several days of burning off, and his son later observed, 'My father had chappies clearing ti tree over there and then we burnt it. There must have been a fair amount of ti tree there because the jokers were clearing it for a long time.'

Unfortunately the fires sometimes got out of hand. Eric Creamer, the son of a keeper, was on Tiri as a young boy from 1910 to 1912. He witnessed 'a great conflagration. ... The fire ... destroyed most of the beautiful natural bush with which it was clad. ... The Marine Department was up in arms about the destruction of some very fine pohutukawa trees. Captain Bollons [captain of the lighthouse tender] had very strong things to say when the *Hinemoa* called a little later.'[5] Another big fire occurred about 1922.

Steedman, when making a valuation in 1908, recorded several buildings at Hobbs Beach (then known as Sandy Bay): a kauri house with chimney and lean-to, the men's house, a wool-shed, sheep yards, fencing, etc. By the 1920s there was also a corrugated-iron shed as storage for the lighthouse station at the beach.

Hobbs also farmed cattle, preferring shorthorns because they were easier to handle after running wild on the island. Transporting the stock was not easy. He writes of putting wool and lambs on the steamer, the *Kotiti*, and also using the *Hinemoa* to send wethers to Shakespear. The Hobbs family later owned the *Vesper*, a 76.8-foot (23.4-metre) scow and *Paradise*, a 20-foot (6-metre) launch.[6] Stock was transported on an open-deck barge with rails around it. One time the overloaded barge overturned. 'All the cattle were drowned except one. We were halfway across the Tiri passage and he swam back to Tiri ... shipping cattle was always a worry ... you would pick the weather as well as you could.'[7]

Water may have been at a premium for the stock. The best stream was the one at the south end of the beach, though nowadays this is just a small trickle into the sand.

Rabbits were abundant on Tiri at the end of the nineteenth

Hobbs' shearing team on Tiri, c.1921. The boy may be Jack Hobbs.
Lola Rae, neé Lord

Left: *Hinemoa*'s boat leaving Tiritiri Matangi, October 1904 (shows a whare and Hobbs' bach behind the beach).
Auckland War Memorial Museum C34728 Buddle album 412

Far left: Hobbs' barge, loaded with cattle.
Daisy Burrell

Facing page: Hobbs' scow, *Vesper*, and launch, *Paradise*, loading stock at Hobbs Beach, 1917.
Daisy Burrell

E. J. (Johnny) Hobbs, Nancy Davies, Daisy and Peggy Hobbs on Tiri, c.1937 (note big concrete water tank behind).
Daisy Burrell

century: when Hobbs went over to shoot them 'the whole hillside used to move with the rabbits'. But they suddenly and mysteriously vanished, with Steedman the ranger reporting in 1908, 'no rabbits now seen on Island, at one time very plentiful'. One theory was that the rabbits had died of a disease, but if so, it must have been one that leaves myxomatosis for dead!

Kiore numbers seem to have been tolerably small during the farming period. There is no mention of them in Hobbs' diaries, and early lighthouse correspondence barely mentions them.

Hobbs' diaries are straightforward records of practical things, with very few lapses into personal matters. In 1893:

> 25 November 1893: Knocking about the house all day doing nothing partikular [sic]. Wasp 'the dog' died today. Great funeral.

And in 1905:

> 10 April: I went up to town from Arkles in the steamer to the Assessment Court.
> 11 April: I was in town all day at the Assessment Court.
> 12 April: Same. Proposed to Daisy Benn and was accepted, and became a respectable engaged man to my sorrow. Amen. W. A little misty rain.

Later in 1905 he permits himself a longer entry:

> 4 December: I was in town all day getting married and Daisy and I came down with the Kotiti and she landed us on her way to Matakana and we had a cup of tea and some cake and oysters.

It is a relief to read that he spent the next day, most uncharacteristically, 'Loafing about all day'.

Johnny and Daisy Hobbs' son, Jack, was born in 1907. When interviewed in 1991 he recalled first being rowed over to Tiri 'as a baby in arms'. Father and son farmed Tiri and Whangaparaoa together.

The lighthouse children enjoyed going down to watch the shearing. Dora Walthew, née King, who lived on Tiri from 1928 to 1936, remembers:

> The people on the island had an arrangement with [Mr Hobbs] to kill an occasional sheep. ... The two hind-quarters went to 2 families and forequarters to the third, changing at the next kill, so every person got a good joint.

> Mr Hobbs would occasionally let his bach to visitors ... [8] We usually met them, as they came up to the station to get free milk.

> We can remember Mr Jack Hobbs bringing his two little girls [Daisy and Peggy] across to the island when he brought a punt load of cattle. They were dressed in little gingham frocks and bonnets and looked lovely.

Daisy Burrell, the daughter of Jack Hobbs, still lives at Whangaparaoa. She remembers playing with the King children, and with Nancy and Bunty Davies who also lived up at the lighthouse.

The 130-year-long farming period had a devastating effect on Tiri's environment, leaving the landscape as barren as on the mainland. The fires will have killed many ground-dwelling birds, lizards and invertebrates. Although the pohutukawa were protected, the manuka and kanuka stands almost disappeared. Goats, in particular, will have had a major effect on the vegetation. Even where tall trees remained in the steepest gullies, they were unfenced. Stock roamed, browsing out the seedlings and low-growing vegetation. Their hooves compressed the ground that had previously been soft and friable, riddled with numerous seabird burrows. Instead of soaking into the soil, heavy rain now ran off, taking with it any leaf litter, and the ground became hard and bare. It has still not recovered from these changes today.

Jack Hobbs took over the farm from his father in about 1938. The stock was removed from the island for the duration of the Second World War. After the war, the farm continued much as before. Johnny Hobbs died in 1947, and in 1961 Peter Arcus became manager. The Crown's yearly rental of £50 had remained the same for the entire lease period. While this was a bargain by

Just a paddock! Tiri in
1936. George Ramsay

1971, it was advantageous to the government to have the island
farmed because it reduced the fire risk.

It had been thought that a last burn-off occurred in 1964,
but letters from Principal Keeper Peter Taylor show that he was
against the intended burn-off because of the number of young
cabbage trees appearing in the grass. Neither Peter Taylor nor
another keeper, Trevor Scott, remembers any burn-offs while
they were on Tiri in the 1950s and 1960s.

The winds of change were blowing: in 1971 Tiritiri Matangi
Island became part of the Hauraki Gulf Maritime Park. After 69
years, the Hobbs family's lease was not renewed, and the stock
was removed, concluding a remarkable era of Tiri's history.

FOUR

ILLUMINATION

The brightness of a lighthouse is measured in candlepower (cp).[1] New Zealand's first 'lighthouse' was a light in a cottage window at Pencarrow, Wellington, in 1849. It was probably a few candle-power. The Tiritiri Matangi lighthouse, built 15 years later, was initially about 1 million cp, but its Davis Marine Light installed in 1965 was 11 million cp.

The story of the Tiri light, its attendants and its attendant structures, is a convoluted one, dominated by the need to keep such a significant lighthouse at the forefront of the latest technology. Powered successively by colza oil, paraffin, acetylene, electricity from diesel generators, a cable link to the national grid, and now by solar-generated electricity, the Tiri light and its accompanying pilot station have guided shipping on the approach to Auckland for 140 years. The lighthouse has been a familiar landmark for generations of recreational sailors. For offshore sailors it has far greater significance, assuring them of landfall after their long voyage.

Auckland was the seat of government from 1840 to 1865, and as shipping traffic increased to the port, it was obvious that a lighthouse and pilot station were needed in the Hauraki Gulf. The New Zealand Government had assumed ownership of Tiritiri Matangi Island as a lighthouse reserve by 1841, but it would be more than 20 years before a lighthouse was built there.

About this time, Captain Thomas Duder went to Tiri with the Auckland harbour master 'to see if it would do for a Pilot Station'. Duder was a signalman who had survived the wreck of HMS *Buffalo* in 1840.[2] On the night of 16 May 1850, the

This early photograph of Tiritiri lighthouse in 1899 was published in the Marine Department annual report. Note the curtains drawn around the light. There is only a small mast at this date.
Auckland War Memorial Museum C31606 Tiritiri lighthouse AJHR 1899 Marine Dept annual report

Facing page: The lighthouse settlement, photographed by Henry Winkelmann in 1902, showing the two original cottages, neatly fenced, the telephone poles, the lighthouse and signal mast with baskets, but no signal tower or plantation trees yet.
Auckland War Memorial Museum C17896 (2380) Winkelmann 1445

Tiri lighthouse, new signal
tower and signal mast,
1913. Tiri Archives

barque *Constantinople,* arriving after a five-month voyage from
England, struck Shearer Rock off Tiritiri Matangi. While the
ship did not sink, the incident further fuelled the calls for a lighthouse: 'Not one light is there to point the benighted Mariner his
path,' trumpeted the *Southern Cross* newspaper (24 May 1850).
'No pilot is placed at a station where his services are of value.' A
report on the incident recommended that 'a light should be
placed on the west point of Tiri Tiri Matanghi [*sic*]'. Although
other locations were also being considered, Tiri was strongly
favoured by the Auckland harbour master Captain Burgess, and
Tiri was included in the Coastal Light Plan of 1861.[3] In that year,
too, the superintendent of Auckland declared that the island
must be reserved as a pilot station.

Designs for the lighthouse were commissioned from the
London engineering firm of Maclean and Stillman, with the
light itself supplied by Chance Brothers, London. The tower was
designed as a prefabricated structure, and on 15 June 1864 the
tower and light arrived in New Zealand on the *Queen of the Deep*
in 279 packages and 36 cases, weighing 75 tons. Twelve bullocks
were barged to the island to haul the cases up on a sledge. The
grass track was so steep and boggy in places that loads of only
half a ton could be pulled at once.

One load must have been lost en route, for a packing case,
dated February 1864, was uncovered by a bulldozer during road-
works in 1956.[4] In *The Sea Is My Neighbour* the keeper, Tom
Clark, wrote that the case was filled with nuts and bolts, but
there's no record that Clark tried to fit the missing components
into the lighthouse. Regrettably, this tale must be taken with a
grain of salt, as Clark was notorious for his tall tales, even in print.

The two keepers' cottages were built first, to provide accommodation for the construction crew. It took the crew four
months to dig down three metres and lay the foundations for
the lighthouse, but construction then proceeded swiftly, the
rectangular cast-iron plates being bolted together like a giant
Meccano set. Each plate is fixed to six adjoining ones for
maximum strength. The assembly was under the supervision of

Richard Aylmer, 'Lighthouse Artificer' for the Marine Board,
who subsequently built two other lighthouses in New Zealand.

The Tiritiri Matangi light was illuminated for the first time
on New Year's Day, 1865 and, as the *Southern Cross* (10 January
1865) reported, 'It had scarcely been lit an hour before the
Barque *Meteor* sighted it at a distance of twenty-six miles . . . it
can be distinctly seen on a clear night from the top of Princes
Street, the Windmill, and other high parts of Auckland.'

The initial light was fixed, not flashing as it is today. The
lamp, with three wicks, burned colza oil (rapeseed or canola oil)
— 'the best quality and carefully strained'. (Captain Burgess
had initially proposed burning sperm-whale oil.) Tanks in the
lower storey of the tower held nine months' supply of fuel, about
1600 litres.

All this fuel had to be transported to Tiri by ship, hauled up
the hill by horse and sled, and pumped up the tower by hand.
Other duties for the keepers included cleaning the lenses, later
winding up the revolving mechanisms every few hours to keep
the lenses turning, trimming the wicks, and drawing the curtains

across in the daytime.[5] At night the powerful Fresnel lenses focused the light into strong, directional beams. By day, without protective curtains, the lenses would focus the sun's rays into the light source and damage it. (The curtains are not needed today because it is a different type of light.)

The lighthouse, which was initially painted bright red, has four storeys, with three windows at each landing. The spiral staircase winds clockwise up the tower, and there is a platform at the top to give access to the light.

The first two keepers were A. Gibson and G. Hand (a list of keepers is in Appendix C). They kept six-hourly watches: one keeper 'lit up' at dusk and stayed up the tower on watch until he was relieved at midnight. The second keeper kept watch till dawn, when he turned off the light, cleaned the lenses and descended, his next task being to milk the family cow. In bad weather a round-the-clock watch was kept.

Five lighthouses were built in New Zealand in 1865[6], and the fledgling Lighthouse Service later put out a manual, *Instructions to Lighthouse Keepers*, which laid out the pedantic rules that were to control the lives of keepers until 1984. 'No parasols to be taken up the lighthouse … Keepers must pay for excessive use of coal. … Interior of houses will be painted French Grey.'

Men entering the lighthouse service were to be between the ages of 21 and 31, 'sober and industrious, cleanly in their persons and habits and orderly in their families. Any flagrant immorality will subject them to immediate dismissal.'

For the keepers, the Lighthouse Service rules controlled everything, with endless logs to be kept and forms to be filled out. There was a Sack Record Book for coal sacks, and a Fog Book to record every day of fog. Some of the routines were time-wasters, designed solely to prevent the keepers from going 'rock happy'. One advantage is that we now have a full record of light-house life: every incoming and outgoing letter was copied into a book. File no. 16, vol. 2 'Earthquake Reports' is empty, save for one letter acknowledging a 1972 report from a Tiri keeper that he had *not* felt a particular earthquake.

Ray Walter describes lighthouse keeping as a 'working class' occupation, yet several keepers have written books: Peter Taylor, Tom Clark, and G. R. Gilbert, who wrote a fictional account of his time on Tiri in *Love in a Lighthouse*. Eric Creamer (the son of a keeper) wrote a lengthy memoir, 'The Tall White Tower', and Mabel (Polly) Pollock, of Devonport, wrote an engaging memoir of her childhood spent at several lighthouses in the 1920s and

Left: Spiral staircase inside the lighthouse, c.1960 (note plates bolted together). Peter Taylor

The lighthouse station from the south, 1935. Tiri Archives

Foghorns

Fog occurs only 10–15 days a year in the vicinity of Tiri.

The first foghorn, a Slaughter's Cotton Powder apparatus, was installed in 1918. The mechanism was brought from Jack's Point, Timaru, after it was deemed to be too loud there (which is not a complaint commonly made about foghorns). On Tiri it was dragged up the hill by bullocks, and installed down the cliffs. The foghorn set off percussive cartridges at intervals. Only a small part of it remains today; the magazine, a solid concrete building that was poured *in situ*, still stands. However, the path down the cliff is unsafe and should not be attempted.

A diaphonic foghorn, operated by compressed air, was installed in 1935. Its large tank was floated across to the island and dragged up the hill by draughthorses. Dora King, then aged 12, watched as the horses were lowered over the side of the ship on a sling, so they could swim ashore. The groom lifted her up onto a horse's back and sent her galloping up the hill in a terrifying ride. Unfortunately no one knows how the horses were loaded back onto the boat afterwards.

Aucklanders remember the moan of this foghorn with nostalgia. Heather Mander, living on Tiri in 1960, thought it sounded like the bellow of a sick cow. It kept her awake at first, but later she only woke up when it was turned off. The diaphonic apparatus is still virtually intact inside the foghorn building, to the south of the lighthouse. Because of its historical value, there are plans to make it operational again as a working model.

On a pole near the foghorn building is the final electronic foghorn, installed in 1983.[7] This was so loud that warning alarms rang when it was about to go off. The noise reached 68 decibels in Ray Walter's bedroom, vibrating the floorboards for one second every minute. But its fog-sensing apparatus was faulty and, since the default position was ON, things got somewhat tense on the island. After it had been switching itself on and off at random for three months, Ray rang the Ministry of Works to complain. They told him to turn it off and Tiri has not had an operating foghorn since. With modern shipping navigation aids it is not deemed necessary.

Top left: Slaughter's gun cotton foghorn, 1921.
Breckon 1921, 4095 Auckland War Memorial Museum

Left: Diaphonic foghorn, 1935.
Tiri Archives

Above: The drum for the diaphonic foghorn, 1935.
Tiri Archives

1930s. However, she never lived on Tiri. One Tiri keeper, Anders Hansen, became an amateur naturalist of note. He had joined the Lighthouse Service on his arrival in New Zealand in 1875 and was on Tiri from 6 August 1906 to 16 November 1909.

The long hours on night watch certainly gave keepers plenty of reading time. They 'were expected to remain awake on duty with only a hard, straight-backed chair to sit on', with lighthouse regulations stipulating that 'chair legs must not be cut down. This is an improper practice and must be discontinued.'[8] Ray Walter explains that taking two inches off chair legs made them into 'easy chairs' that, when tilted back, were more comfortable to sit on. 'Peculiarly, the light that could be seen for miles by sea-farers was only just bright enough to read a book by inside the light room.'[9]

Eric Creamer describes a keeper on watch: 'wrapped up against the cold of the unheated iron tower, wearing a heavy overcoat, a balaclava and a thick pair of ankle length slippers'. He boiled his billy by hanging it over the lamp chimney.[10]

The Tiri light was converted to paraffin oil in 1880. This was so flammable that the Dangerous Goods Act 1869 required it to be stored at least 50 metres from other buildings. Consequently two small storage sheds were built near the gate to the lighthouse station: one contained drums of flammable materials while the other stored the signal flags that were flown from the tall mast to communicate with ships. (See 'Signals', page 39.)

In 1882 a red glass plate was fitted to the Tiri light, creating a 'sectored' light to warn shipping of Flat Rock, near Kawau Island. A ship heading down the coast towards Tiri, but on track for the rock, saw a red light rather than the usual white one from the lighthouse.[11] This red pane was removed in 1922 after Flat Rock got its own danger beacon.

In 1916 a pressurised system was introduced that burned kerosene using a mantle, similar to a Coleman lantern. This gave a brilliant incandescent light, but the system had to be pumped up every three hours. (Kerosene and paraffin are essentially the same oil.)

'THE QUEEN STREET LIGHT'

In comparison to other lighthouse stations such as bleak Puysegur Point, or isolated Moko Hinau, Tiritiri Matangi was considered an easy posting, having a benign climate and Auckland city close by. Other keepers scathingly described Tiri as 'the light at the end of Queen's Wharf' or 'the Queen Street Light'.

Using her father's huge telescope, Betty King, the youngest daughter of Chief Signalman Alf King, could even read the time from the clock on Auckland's Ferry Building and, looking eastwards, she could pick out the ships passing Cuvier Island.

'Everyone wanted to go to Tiri,' says Ray Walter, the last lighthouse keeper on Tiri, but his daughter Lynda, in the 1970s, took another view:

> Throughout my childhood whenever we travelled home to Moko Hinau, Tiri was the first island stop, and it was so close to Auckland it seemed like the trip had only just begun. I don't think I ever really thought of it as a 'real' lighthouse station. I can remember the first time I saw Tiri when I was seven and we were travelling to Moko Hinau on the *Colville* on transfer from Castlepoint. I had been told by Mum and Dad that we were going to live on an island, and I can remember my teacher at Castlepoint school making a fuss about me going to live on an island far out in the sea. When we got to Tiri I was a bit worried in case we had arrived at our new home because it didn't seem far enough away from the mainland for me!

Families in the Lighthouse Service were rotated to a new posting every few years. When the Walter family shifted to Tiri in 1980, Lynda Walter found the relative civilisation unsettling after Moko Hinau:

> Tiri was a bit of a shock to me because there were lots of other people around to help out, we had a tractor and electricity and a telephone. I found it hard to cope with the idea that people visited the island for picnics and for all sorts

One of the two storage sheds, in its later guise as a schoolroom. Fourteen-year-old Lola Lord and her pupils, 1921 (see page 45).
Lola Rae, neé Lord

A keeper once fell on the stairs inside the lighthouse. He slipped through the railings and hung by his arm for some time before he was found and rescued.[12]

Captain John Bollons,
May 1904.
Auckland War Memorial
Museum. Album 412-1

Below: The lighthouse
tender, GSS *Hinemoa*.
Auckland War Memorial
Museum. Album 412-1

of other reasons that had nothing to do with the running of the lighthouse station.

Nevertheless the families on the island had to plan well to eke out their provisions, especially in the early days when the supply ships called only every three months as they worked a circuit of the lighthouses. Bad weather could mean delays, and while the families usually had enough food in reserve, a shortage of tobacco was felt most keenly. All the supplies were ordered ahead of time from Farmers' Trading Co. and Hellaby's Meats. Phoned orders often got scrambled: keepers got soap in place of rope, tea instead of cheese — and vice versa.[13]

The Marine Board first used a paddle steamer, the *Luna*, to supply the lighthouses, but after 1876 the elegant sister ships *Stella* and *Hinemoa* were designed specifically for lighthouse work. The latter was commanded by the legendary Captain John Bollons (1862–1929), 'a fluent Maori speaker, resourceful master seaman, tough disciplinarian and a kind hearted gentleman'.[14] He was young Eric Creamer's hero. In 'The Tall White Tower', Creamer, who was on Tiri from 1910 to 1912, recalls his childhood living at lighthouses. 'I find it quite impossible to

remember the *Hinemoa* coming to anchor off one of the lighthouse-stations … without visualising Captain John Bollons, her Master, on the Bridge, Mr. Jackson, the Chief Engineer, in his engine-room … '

Bernard Fergusson, the son and grandson of New Zealand governors, and later a governor-general himself, sailed with Captain Bollons at age 14:

> In appearance he was broad and stocky … with startling blue eyes and a grey pointed beard, always neatly trimmed … At sea and ashore, he used always to stand with his hands behind his back and his feet well apart, as though to anticipate a roll of the ship even though on land. … I recall his coming to tea at Government House, when my mother asked anxiously whether he might not have got wet in the sudden rain squall which had smitten us all a few minutes before. 'Oh, no, Your Excellency,' he replied; 'I hove to under the lee of the Post Office.'[15]

BOAT DAYS

Boat days were holidays. The Lighthouse Service captains were the island's contact with the outside world. They brought the latest news, especially gossip from other lighthouses. Nancy Davies wrote for the Correspondence School in 1929:

> Mail day is a very busy day at Tiri. Early in the morning Mum gets all the lessons and all the letters ready to put in the mail bag … Then Dad and Mr. King get the horse and sleigh ready. When they hear the launch has left town, they go down the track to the beach. If my lessons are done Mum lets me go down, too.

Initially, goods were landed at Hobbs Beach, but by 1909 a short wooden wharf was built at the site of the present wharf.[16]

To transport the goods, the station horse pulled the 'konaki', a sled with runners at the front and one set of wheels at the back. G. R. Gilbert's first attempts to drive the konaki were a disaster:

he soon discovered that if one went too fast on the downhill run, the horse would end up being run over by the sled.[17]

John, the grey draughthorse, was there before 1918. 'He was very easy to catch as he knew at the end of the day he would receive [as] his reward a thick slice of bread liberally coated with treacle or golden syrup.'[18] When he was retired in the 1930s, a new horse, Tommy, arrived. 'He was a half draught horse, and was very nervous and hard to manage.'[19] 'Everyone remembers Tommy.'[20] 'He was a great old horse.'[21] Tommy was still there in 1959, having terrorised keepers and their families for over 20 years. Even the navy couldn't tame him. (See Chapter 5, 'On Active Service'.)

> This was the day the family had fresh meat for tea ...
> All other meats had to be put down in brine. All the family shared with the unpacking and putting away the goods. Tinned meats and fish. Large sacks of flour and sugar. Dried fruits, cereals, dried peas ... Seven pound tins of treacle and golden syrup, four and a half pound tins of biscuits.[22]

In G. R. Gilbert's time, it was 'Christmas once a fortnight' when the boat came. Two weeks' worth of newspapers arrived at once.

In Gilbert's novel, his fictional Principal Keeper, 'Mr Ratchett', read one newspaper a day, starting with the oldest, to keep them in sequence, but the Gilberts impetuously ripped open the most recent first, and made do with stale news until the next boat.[23]

If the ship carried passengers, they came ashore during the lengthy unloading period and walked up to the lighthouse. Mrs King had several sets of fine china cups, saucers and plates. 'These came out on boat days only, to entertain any visitors. Lovely crochet mats on the sideboard ... Bright cushions on settee, lace curtains at window. Table and chairs in centre of room. Red velvet cloth on table and a vase of flowers in centre of table.'[24] The visitors were served tea with wonderful home baking.

This tradition continued to the end: in the early 1980s, Ray Walter's wife, Val, was famed for her baking. When she saw the supply boat approaching across the Gulf, she knew she had time to put a cake and a batch of scones in the oven. Her cakes were filled with lashings of whipped cream from the station's cows. While this was usually greatly appreciated by visitors, Neil

Left: John, the grey draughthorse, pulling a load on the konaki, 1918.
Joan Bates, née Roberts/ Tiri Archives

John near the pa site, c.1921. Note the wharf and the bare terrain.
Lola Rae, neé Lord

Members of the Lyon family outside the Principal Keeper's House, 1921. Mrs Lyon crocheted a tablecloth every year to commemorate her wedding anniversary.
Lola Rae, née Lord

SS *Triumph* on the rocks at Tiri, 1883.
4-1439 SS *Triumph* at Tiritiri Matangi 1883. Auckland City Libraries

Mitchell of the University of Auckland recalls a dreadfully rough trip out with a television crew, when almost everyone was seasick. With the visitors still feeling green on their arrival at the top of the hill, the last thing they wanted was whipped cream.

SHIPWRECKS

The Rev. John Bumby drowned when his 37-foot waka overturned between Rakino and Tiri on 6 June 1840. This is the first recorded wreck near Tiri.[25]

On 29 November 1883 the 1797-ton steamer *Triumph*, on her maiden voyage from England, left Auckland for Wellington. It was a clear night, and the captain went below to sleep, instructing the helmsman to 'steer for the Tiri light'. This he did with great accuracy, getting to within a kilometre of the lighthouse before running the ship onto the Pinnacles rocks.[26] There was no loss of life but, while the officers were taken off the island, the Chinese crew was left to camp for two months on a beach, known since then as Chinamans Bay. The *New Zealand Herald* (2 January 1884) advertised: 'At the request of numbers of Ladies and Gentlemen who are desirous of visiting the wreck of the SS *Triumph*, the company will run their Powerful steamer *Waitaki*, Today Tuesday at 2 o'clock … return fare four shillings.' The *Triumph* was salvaged in January 1884.

One person drowned when the 598-ton barque *Royal Tar* sank on 14 December 1908 after striking Shearer Rock. This 'submerged rock' is a major shipping hazard. It now has a cardinal warning marker with a beacon.

Eric Creamer described how his father 'averted a shipwreck' near Shearer Rock in about 1911. 'A large steamer was approaching from the north-west, about to pass between Shearer Buoy and Tiri Tiri.' Rushing to the signal mast, the keeper put up a flag signal: *'You are running on to danger'*. 'For a brief space of time the steamer continued on her course and then suddenly she began to turn.' The ship did a 180-degree turn and headed back out to sea at speed.[27]

SIGNALS

Tiritiri Matangi was probably a pilot station from the time of the lighthouse construction, but communicating with vessels was essentially a separate function from the lighthouse activity. The first keepers had a 'signal staff which will give [them] immediate communication' with Auckland in case of a mishap, and by 1885, at least, the signal station was in operation.[28]

By day, signal flags were flown from a mast (which was taller than the lighthouse) while at night Morse code was sent by signal lamp, 'which has enabled messages to be sent to a steamer 10 miles distant'.[29] At night, ships would send up flares and rockets to attract the signalman's attention. The large wicker shapes seen in the photographs were used to communicate with the mainland before there was a telegraphic link, since the distance was too great for flag signals.

Signal flags are still used internationally by ships at sea to spell out short messages. Tiri's signals usually concerned whether a pilot was required, but some messages, possibly from a ship that had been out of communication with the land for months, had more urgency:

11 Feb 1907 *Port Elgin* from North
'Captain is sick
Surgeon wanted'

23 May 1907 Barque *Manurewa*
'I have been in collision with ketch
Want a tug'[30]

The messages were transmitted from Tiri to the Auckland port authorities by various methods over the years: back in 1885 all it required was a telephone call, after a cable had been laid to the island. As the *Evening Post* reported in 1931: 'great was the excitement on the station when word was received in March 1885 that war had been declared with Russia and to keep a look-out for any large steamers.'

A keeper or signalman, possibly Mr Lyon, in 1921. A posed photo: the telescope would normally be inside the signal tower, and the large signal baskets were no longer used as there was a telephone link to the mainland.
Breckon 1921, 4093 Auckland War Memorial Museum

Peter Taylor salvaged this Tiri signals log book. Here the signalman has recorded the arrival of the 'Great White Fleet' on 9 August 1908: 'American Squadron, 16 battleships'. Anne Rimmer

The Morse House in 1913.
Tiri Archives

Far right: The present
signal tower was initially
a one-storey building,
c.1912. Daisy Burrell

Signalman Henry Dunnet
outside the signal tower,
1938. Judith Lord, née Dunnet

Auckland businessmen had donated funds to lay the underwater cable from Waiwera to Tiri. The line terminated in a small octagonal telephone booth on the slopes south of the lighthouse. 'It was all glass apart from the doorway.'[31] This charming folly, with its curved pagoda roof, appears in only six known photographs. It looks better suited to a city park than a remote island.

However, the 'Morse House', as it was known, proved a folly in operation as well as design. The signalmen were supposed to report the arrival of the packet steamer bringing the mail, which arrived off Tiri about 5 a.m. But the Auckland telegraph office did not open till 9 a.m., by which time the packet had already berthed. The telephone line was still operating in 1928 but 'it was lost in a heavy storm not long after'.[32] Subsequently the signalmen communicated by Morse code.

In 1908 the Auckland Harbour Board 'erected a signal-house for the shelter of the keepers when on the look-out for vessels'.[33] Intriguingly, one faded early photo shows the signal-house as one storey high, not two storeys high, as it is today. In 1912 it became compulsory for all vessels arriving at Auckland to take on a pilot to guide them into port, and two AHB signalmen were stationed on Tiri to signal to the ships as they approached. The pilot boat met the ships near Rangitoto Island.

Two houses were erected in 1912 for the signalmen. One-upmanship between the AHB and the Lighthouse Service may have inspired the elegant Chief Signalman's House with its beautiful garden on the eastern cliffs. Spring bulbs and pink *Amaryllis* lilies still appear in the grass near the lighthouse. Certainly the signalmen considered themselves a cut above the lighthouse keepers.

For the assistant signalman, the 'Fourth House', a 'large rambling wooden home of 5 bedrooms', was brought over from Greys Ave in Auckland and erected south of the lighthouse, looking out to The Noises group.[34] Lola Lord lived there in 1920–21 while her father was assistant signalman.

The Auckland Harbour Board went out to inspect their new signal station in 1913, the *New Zealand Herald* (8 August 1913) reporting: 'The island, at its summit, is now assuming a settled appearance, there being four cottages for the lighthouse keeper and his assistants, and the signal station men.' And at night, there were two men on watch: a keeper up in the lighthouse and a signalman in the signal-house, or Watchtower as it is known today.

In 1925 a flashing acetylene light was installed in the lighthouse. Flashing lights are preferable to fixed ones because they cannot be confused with other lights around. Since the new light was automatic, the lighthouse keepers were withdrawn, and the Auckland Harbour Board took over the administration of Tiri, with three signalmen manning the signal station.

Both the Lighthouse Service and the AHB required their staff to be married. (Henry Dunnet, in 1938, had to get married in order to take up the signalman's position on Tiri.) The AHB staff were not rotated to other islands as the lighthouse keepers had been, so, for example, the Davies family lived on Tiri from 1928 to 1939, while the King family was there from 1928 to 1936. The old Fourth House was now empty, and the King children played ghosts in it.

A strict hierarchy was observed at lighthouse stations. The families met only on special occasions, and as G. R. Gilbert writes, an invitation to afternoon tea with the principal keeper and his wife called for him to have a special shave and don a suit.[35] It was the same with the AHB, partly because so many of the families were ex-Navy.

Even the children socialised formally. In 1929, Pat King wrote for the Correspondence School: 'The day in the week I like best is Saturday, because a little girl named Nancy [Davies] asks me up to tea. I go up in the afternoon at two o'clock and play until tea-time. On fine days we play in the backyard. On wet days we play indoors. When it is seven o'clock I go home.'

THE DARKER SIDE

But it wasn't all china cups and doilies. Accidents were inevitable in this rugged island environment: John, the horse, fell to his death after he was retired, and two tractors went over in later years, though no one was hurt.[36] Little Bunty Davies almost went over the cliff too! 'While Mr Davies was bringing stores from the boatshed [the horse] took fright and bolted down past our house with Bunty in the sledge,' remembers Dora King. 'Mr Davies could not hold him and lost the reins. We all thought Bunty and the sledge had gone over the cliff when they disappeared from view. But the sledge tipped just short of the cliff and Bunty fell out. It gave us all a dreadful fright.'[37] In the mid-1950s, Stan Rhodes fell down the cliffs while taking his sons fishing, knocking himself unconscious.

Island life was perhaps especially hard on the women:

Mum used to bake bread every day … She would raise the bread on the rack above the stove … my brother Alf was leaning above the stove and put his weight on the rack. It all fell forward and he fell with his face on the hot stove and had terrible burns. He was nicknamed Grill Chops for quite a long time. As well as being capable at everything, most parents had to be Doctors as well. Dad always had a good medicine cabinet. The chief remedy being castor oil which we received in liberal doses. Every Saturday morning we had to take a dose of sulphur and treacle for a general tonic. It must have worked as we never seemed to suffer much sickness.[38]

Newlywed Mrs Hilda Dunnet (below) with her sister Millicent on the signal-mast ladder, 1938.
Judith Lord, née Dunnet

Left: The lighthouse station in 1912. Ten years after Winkelmann's photo, the signal tower has been built and the plantation is obscuring the houses.
Alexander Turnbull Library, Wellington F32650½

Tiri from the sea, showing the foghorn down the cliff, the Morse House, 'Fourth House', signal tower, lighthouse and Principal Keeper's house, c.1921.
Tiri Archives

Expectant mothers went to the mainland to await their confinement, but one baby wouldn't wait: Tiri Gow was born on Tiritiri Matangi in 1920. Mrs Tiri Bourke, née Gow, attended the Tiri reunion in 2003. She is very proud of her name. The only other child known to have been named after the island is Tiri Fowler, who was born in about 1968, the son of keeper Roger Fowler and his wife, Chris.

A distressing accident occurred on the island on Monday, 14 December 1880, when Alfred Leith, a young son of the assistant keeper, fell over the highest cliff on the island and was killed. The keepers were unable to get down the cliff to the unfortunate lad, and endeavoured then to go round in the lighthouse boat, which got stove in on the rocks in the big sea running. Signals were sent to Auckland for the police launch, but although the launch reached the island no one could land until the Friday, when the body was taken to Auckland for burial.[39]

SELF-SUFFICIENCY

Water was scarce in summer. There was a deep 60-metre well near the lighthouse. It went down almost to sea level and the water was very hard. Big rectangular concrete tanks collected water from the house roofs, but even so, water shortages occurred every year.

Each family had extensive vegetable gardens sited down in the gullies where the soil was better. Remains of stone walls beside the wharf toilets show the location of one of these gardens. The animals — sheep, pigs, ducks, hens and cows — were kept up at the lighthouse station. Milking a cow was a challenge for some new keepers, and 'townies' could not cope with the conditions. 'Nothing equipped my mother for life on Tiri,' remembers Agnes Hagan, née Petty, who was on Tiri briefly in 1939. She recalls her mother's bread, which 'was a disaster and went over the cliff in disgust', and her father's distaste at having to catch and kill a fowl. 'Looking back, one sees the humour. I doubt Dad had killed anything bigger than a mouse. The axe, chopping block, and a look of utter disgust. That was when I learnt chooks kept running after losing their heads and we had to search for them.'

When it became too much, Agnes' father hailed a passing fishing boat and her mother escaped to Auckland, taking their youngest child with her until the supply boat was due back again.

Newlywed Mrs Hilda Dunnet in 1938 sometimes went into Auckland 'surrounded by live crayfish in a small boat', and when Alfie King ran away from boarding school his father received a radio message late at night from a fishing boat: 'I have your son on board, will land him in the morning at the wharf.'[40]

Young Susan Lyon loved being on Tiri. She came out from Scotland in 1911 to live with her uncle, keeper Joseph Lyon. She developed such affection for the island that when she returned home in 1918 to marry, she modelled her new house in Saltcoats, Ayrshire, on the old keepers' cottages and named it Tiri Tiri.

Fishing

Fishing was a popular pastime, augmenting the families' supplies of tinned and salted meats. 'Fishing for my father was like what one hears at a lying competition,' boasted Eric Creamer. 'Father shot a shag, baited the hook with a piece of flesh and tossed the line into the water. Soon he would have landed all the large schnapper he required. (That was before the trawlers started.)'[41]

Dora King remembers a remarkable sight on the eastern side: 'One stormy day my brother Reg and I were walking around the rocks and in a wide crevice we saw all types of fish which had come in from the stormy waters. There were young snapper, terakihi, herring, pink mau mau and several other types. We just watched in amazement. We never ever saw it again. They were just swimming about as though they were at a party.'[42]

G. R. Gilbert discovered a novel use for surplus fish: he had tried salting some fish and hung them up to dry, but no one wanted to eat them. However, they made a pretty reliable weather guide, being dry and hard when the outlook was good, but if they were soft and puffy a change for the worse was on the way.[43]

The 'new' lower house, now the bunkhouse, c.1960. Trevor Scott

Below left: Visitors, in 1921, caught 200 snapper in one day. Lola Rae, née Lord

TWO NEW HOUSES

'Rain has fallen every day this month so far. It seems if we were to have no summer. Surely the weather is quite abnormal,' wrote Anders Hansen in October 1907, and two years later: 'Through being crippled in my right knee with rheumatism I haven't been able to get about the island for a long time.'[44]

The original keepers' cottages had also suffered in Tiri's rugged weather, and were in poor repair by the First World War. Two new keepers' houses were built in 1918 — they are the present DOC officers' house and the bunkhouse. They originally had three bedrooms, and half-verandas on their western faces, but both houses have been modified.

Outside each house was a wood store, laundry and the toilet — a wooden bench with a hole and a cover, with a kerosene tin underneath. 'Toilet paper was the *Weekly News* cut up into 6-inch squares.'[45] The children got 'the hated job (usually done on a wet day), of emptying the toilet tin over the cliff edge. They would put a stout stick through the handle and, clad in grain-sack hoods … they proceeded like monks down the paddock, carrying the offending matter to the edge of the cliff.'[46] There was a surplus of kerosene tins and they were used for everything.

Up until the 1950s the houses were lit by kerosene lamp. In the 1920s the houses had telephones with handles (one is used in the shop today!), but the phone connection was lost when the cable to the mainland broke. Cooking was done on a stove that burned both coal and wood. Lighthouse regulations stipulated that torn coal sacks must be mended before being returned on the next boat.[47]

Correspondence School

'The Correspondence School had not been long in operation and we were some of the first pupils to enrol,' explains Dora King. 'The schoolwork was sent out each fortnight in large blue double-flapped envelopes with the addresses on each side. When the work was returned the flap would cover the sender's name and address.' The children's mother supervised their schoolwork for about four hours each morning.

The Correspondence School was opened in 1922 with 100 pupils initially, and had 720 students on the roll by 1927. Many Lighthouse Service children were on the roll, as were the AHB signalmen's children on Tiri. Dora King remembers: 'The arrival of the stores boat brought marked schoolwork plus the new set of lessons. When the task of putting away the stores was done, the next task was the

Peeps at Tiri Tiri.
By NANCY DAVIES, Std. I.

———

My Island Home.

I love to roam among the rocks
And hear the sea birds call,
Or spade in hand I dig the sand,
And watch my castles fall.

I love to paddle in the sea
In glorious summer time;
The sun is strong the whole day
   long,
I crave no other clime.

LEAVE

Lighthouse keepers couldn't take weekends and holidays like 'normal' people. They were employed for 40 hours a week over seven days. After working 360 consecutive days they got 32 consecutive days' leave, during which a relieving keeper replaced them.

Annual leave was the highlight of the year, with everything focused towards it for months beforehand. 'Such a bloody sewing undoing of the school envelopes, to see just how many mistakes one had in their set. Also, to read the remarks from the teachers in Wellington.'

The children on Tiri wrote stories and poems for the December 1929 edition of *The Postman*. There was great excitement when the edition arrived on Tiri.

> If you came to Tiri, I would take you up to the top of the Lighthouse so that you could see how the light worked. After that I would take you to the outside platform, and you could see the sea for miles and miles. Then we would take a walk to the signal tower and Dad would tell you about the signals and wireless and show you the engine room, because I am not allowed to go in there. Then we would go home for lunch before going down to the fog signal which is a long way down the cliff. Dad would let a shot go from the signal gun so that you could hear what a noise it makes, and you could have a peep at the powder magazine. Then we would come home to have tea.[48]

Agnes Petty in 1939 did her schoolwork in the office at the base of the lighthouse; Peter Rhodes in the 1950s did his in the 'Fog House' (the diaphonic foghorn building), which, if you think about it, was a quiet place on most days of the year; and in the 1980s Lynda Walter practised for her School Certificate exam by typing letters for her father in the Watchtower. Ray had acquired an old electric typewriter from a bank. It wasn't the best — the letter 'a' kept falling off, and Lynda had to wear gumboots while typing because the machine gave her shocks.

Nancy Davies on the lighthouse's platform, 1929. *The Postman*

and knitting. Teaching the kids to behave and getting them used to wearing shoes again,' says Ray Walter.

But ironically the longed-for leave often turned sour. Having no immunity to them, families caught the current cold or flu bugs as soon as they returned to civilisation. And, after being accustomed to silence and fresh sea air, some found the sounds and smells of the city intolerable.[49] More than one family returned home to their island sanctuary earlier than they had intended.[50]

A WHOLESOME LIFE

For the children, life on Tiri seems to have been a carefree existence, except, in some cases, for an authoritarian father. The little Mander children were playing quietly indoors one rainy day. Their mother found them sitting cross-legged on the floor rocking from side to side. Richard, the eldest, said they were being 'flashing light buoys'. 'And girls!' piped up little Ruth.[51]

Before the Correspondence School started in 1922, Lola Lord, though only 14, received special permission to be school-mistress to four young children on the station. One of the small

sheds was used as the schoolroom. 'They used to stand outside and do toothbrush drill — you could spit anywhere.'[52]

Lola, who was keen on photography, discovered she could crawl under the by-then disused Morse House to develop her films in that dark space. A few years later the three younger King children 'discovered the manhole in the ceiling' of the Morse House, and hid up there when they were being called to do chores, something their elder sister Pat — who had searched for them — learned only during their interview with the author in 2003.

The King children got up to some amazing pranks: catching Mr Hobbs' mare, Venus, and riding her bareback; and launching the station dinghy and rowing it around, always under the cliffs where their father, up at the lighthouse, couldn't see them. They built a playhouse from flotsam and jetsam at Northeast Bay (over two kilometres from the lighthouse), where they cooked oysters

The Roberts and Lyon families posed in the lifeboat, 1918.
Joan Bates, née Roberts/ Tiri Archives

Left: The King children and Nancy Davies with the signal baskets, c.1928. Pat Meyer, née King

'We had a wholesome life.'
– Dora Walthew, née King

45

Fantail

'Small pockets of bush grew in the gullies and many varieties of birds lived there.'[53]

Often the first bird to approach visitors on Tiri is the lively fantail. Its endearing habit of escorting walkers, squeaking excitedly, is due not to affection but to the fact that our movement stirs up tiny insects for this little flycatcher to eat: if you listen closely you can hear its beak snap. Fantails follow

saddlebacks for the same reason, moving through the bush at a slightly lower level in order to intercept any dislodged insects.

The fan-shaped tail assists its remarkable aerobatics; yet several tail-less fantails have been seen on Tiri in recent years — and very comical truncated things they are. But their tail-less state does not affect their manoeuvrability; if anything, they are even better acrobats than their normal counterparts. Whether the lack of a tail is genetic or just a complete moult is not known.

In the winter of 2002 a flock of about 15 fantails stayed around the lighthouse area. It was a treat to see the flurry of excited children and fantails, the birds continually alighting right at the children's feet but never being trodden on.

A hundred years earlier the lighthouse keeper Anders Hansen had written:

' ... Very few birds strike this tower and are hardly ever killed. I shall keep a note, in future, of all birds striking. The pied fantail sometimes comes on summer nights to collect moths on the lantern panes, of which they reap a fine harvest on still, dark nights.' Hansen would surely have enjoyed the scene almost 100 years later, at the base of his lighthouse.

Above: A tail-less fantail. Anne Rimmer
Left: A normal fantail. Peter Craw

Nancy Davies riding John, c.1936. Lola Rae, née Lord

and mussels along with vegetables stolen from the garden and jellies from the larder, '1 pound of dates stuffed up the bloomer leg'.[54] These they served up in style: 'Sometimes plates from passing steamers [the *Mariposa* and the *Monterey*] found their way ashore and these were carefully placed on the rocky shelves in the driftwood hut.'[55]

Lynda Walter says: 'I suppose I was one of the last kids to have a lighthouse childhood, and the pattern of activity seems to have been much the same whether you were born in 1905 or 1965.'

~

FIVE

ON ACTIVE SERVICE

War was declared on Sunday, 3 September 1939, and 12 members of the Royal New Zealand Naval Volunteer Reserve (RNZNVR) arrived on Tiri the next day. Unfortunately their supplies didn't! Malcolm Kay remembered:

> When they put us in this launch to send us down to Tiri, we had a cut lunch, and they said there is a barge coming down with either 3 months' or 6 months' provisions. When we got up to the signal tower eventually, we spotted this barge being towed down towards the island, but there was such a howling gale that it went over into Whangaparaoa to get shelter. The tug couldn't hold it and it got washed ashore. Of course there was all our supplies, and the head lighthouse keeper … the Davies family, they fed the 12 of us for 3½ days.[1]

War had been expected for some time, and these were well-trained men; Malcolm Kay, for example, had been in the Reserves for eight years. They came to Tiri to man a Port War Signal Station (PWSS) which would identify every ship approaching Auckland. They had no armaments whatsoever.

Tiri had not been the obvious location for the PWSS. It was thought to be too far out, with weather problems and difficulties in supply, misgivings that were immediately proven correct with the mishap to the RNZNVR barge. When the weather eased the barge was refloated and towed over to Tiri, but then the men had to get their supplies up the hill:

> We had to use that konaki and that ruddy horse Tommy — temperamental thing it was. I think the poor old horse

wondered what had hit it, having to go up and down, up and down. Of course this konaki didn't hold such a terrible lot of stuff and you would take 70 lb bags of flour and 70 lbs of sugar and boxes of tea. We had to go and get Nancy, the head lighthouse keeper's daughter, she was the only one who could catch him. She would take a piece of bread coated with sugar out to him. Bribery!²

As the only single young woman on the island, Nancy Davies would have been a magnet for the young sailors.

The Petty family were still on Tiri when war was declared. Twelve-year-old Agnes Petty watched from the cliffs as a large enemy raider sailed into the Hauraki Gulf. It cruised past Tiri, circled and went away. Sixty-five years later she still remembers the sight vividly. Agnes' family left Tiri in October 1939.

Ships at sea were forbidden to use their wireless in wartime, so communication with them was by flags, semaphore or Aldis signal lamps. From Tiri to Auckland, signal lamps, radio, or later a telephone line, were used. A message could go from Tiri–Rangitoto–North Head–Naval Defence HQ, Mount Eden in three minutes. Some ships were a bit slow to catch on. The *Matua*, coming in from the islands a few days after war was declared, did not respond to Tiri's request for identification, nor to another from the Examination Steamer (an old boat anchored off Rangitoto) — so the guns at Narrow Neck landed a shell in front of her. 'That soon woke them up!'³

The Navy was duplicating much of the AHB work of identification. At first the two services shared the AHB facilities,

'Wiggy' Bennett on the signal-tower steps, 1939.
Malcolm Kay

W. R. Harrison in front of Fourth House, with the derelict Morse House to the left, 1939. Malcolm Kay

Right: The mast and Fourth House from up the lighthouse, 1939. Malcolm Kay

Far right: The Port War Signal Station building, c.1940. Malcolm Kay

but it soon became apparent that the navy needed its own building. The officer in charge, W. R. Harrison, put out a directive: 'All ratings … are forbidden to visit the Harbour Board houses or to discuss their work, or personnel, outside the station. Attention is drawn to the confidential nature of their work.' Harrison was commonly known as 'Crash' Harrison. Every serviceman had a nickname: Bluey, Shorty, Nobby, Wiggy.

The Navy's living quarters were dreadful. The men were put in the Fourth House, that 'old dunger', which 'wasn't fit for human habitation'.[4] It was dirty, tumbledown and leaking — the men slept with oilskins over their bedding in order to stay dry. And to cap it all, the house was haunted:

During the night … you would hear somebody shuffling up the passage like the old Chinese habit of shuffling. Of course Crash Harrison, he used to yell out 'Who's there?' Of course he wouldn't get any answer and in the morning he would question the blokes because they knew darn well, going by the time, that the bloke who was on watch would have been in the signal tower, and so he couldn't have come down to get in, and nobody would walk like that. … when they questioned some of the other lighthouse keepers, they said,

'Oh, didn't they tell you? It's an old house from Greys Avenue — belonged to some old Chinese, and it is haunted.'[5]

It is worth noting that these were practical, disciplined military men, not the sort of people one might expect to be affected by ghosts.

Following several official visits and subsequent reports about the substandard accommodation — even the medical officer became involved — materials were barged in to build the Port War Signal Station, an imposing white building of about 43 by 24 feet (13 x 7 metres), which stood to the south of the lighthouse. This provided accommodation, as well as some working space. The PWSS had a fine view from Kawau Island past Great Barrier and the Coromandel to Auckland but, significantly, the Tiri channel was obscured.

The young naval ratings were rotated regularly, usually being sent overseas as signalmen with ships sailing in convoys. On 17 April 1940, three of them went sailing in the Tiri channel. They didn't return. 'We went up to the top of the lighthouse to see if we could see them,' Malcolm Kay remembered, 'and there was no sign of them.' The three men drowned were Jack William

Dallow, aged 20, Des C. Waite and W. A. Ryan. Only Dallow's body was found.

Malcolm Kay and Nancy Davies were married on 21 September 1940. Malcolm left Tiri in 1940 and joined the *Achilles*. About a month later, the *Niagara* was sunk by a German mine 48 kilometres off the New Zealand coast to the north of Tiri.

After the bombing of Pearl Harbor (7 December 1941), the US poured money into New Zealand defences and the Army established a Fortress Observation Post (FOP) on Tiri. The Army rebuilt the Fourth House, concreting the outside and adding a concrete tower, which was painted cream with a red roof to match the lighthouse buildings. Only four or five army personnel were on the island at a time. Major L. H. Titchener, Ninth Coastal Battery, was officer in charge from 1940 to 1944. The FOP gave information to the nine-inch guns on Whangaparaoa Peninsula and controlled the mines in the Tiri channel, which could be exploded by pressing a button on shore. The mines laid from Tiri to Rakino and The Noises were contact mines, which exploded when struck by a ship.

With the arrival of the Army, the AHB signalmen were withdrawn, leaving one man as custodian of the foghorn and radio beacon.

The Port War Signal Station building was dismantled in 1942 and rebuilt halfway along the island, a location from which the Tiri channel could be seen. In the channel was a 'loop' cable, which indicated if a ship or submarine passed over it. A Japanese submarine 'pinged' this loop both coming and going. There was also a degaussing range in the channel, which demagnetised ships' hulls, making them less susceptible to mines. The cables were removed in the 1960s. A mobile radar unit was to be set up on Tiri but it did not eventuate.

The move of the PWSS to its new location was the end as far as Tommy, the horse, was concerned. One can imagine the chagrin of the writer of this official letter:

From Naval Officer in Charge, Auckland District. To the Naval Secretary, Wellington. 12 March 1943.

Since commissioning the station in September 1939, the naval personnel at Tiri Tiri have made use of the Auckland Harbour Board's horse which, for fifteen years, has hauled stores from the landing jetty to the vicinity of the lighthouse.

Malcolm Kay and
Nancy Davies, 1940.
Judith Lord, née Dunnet

Above right: The wharf
was a much busier place
in wartime, especially
when materials were
shipped in for the two
large buildings, c.1940.
Malcolm Kay

This animal is not only vicious but obstinate to such a degree that no amount of persuasion or coercion by the entire personnel of the island will induce him to cover the additional half-mile to the new PWSS. ... Approval is sought for the purchase of a more suitable horse at an estimated cost of £25.[6]

Since, by 1943, five tons of stores were arriving monthly, one can hardly blame Tommy for objecting. Even water in 10-gallon casks had to be shipped in, and the large, round concrete tank behind the nursery is probably a wartime construction. Not before time, tractors were finally brought to the island.

The Hobbs family had taken their stock off the island in 1940, donating a cow to each of the services. Now, as the grass grew higher, the kiore rats increased to plague numbers. The Army rigged up a high-voltage electric fence around the FOP, with a small light on the wall that lit up every time a rat was zapped. Although it killed thousands, the fence did not make a dent in the kiore population. The Navy had a more low-tech solution: 'Bluey' Wheldale 'pinched a tom cat from the Naval Base one day and drafted him to Tiri for anti-rat duties. Frank Canny operated on him and made him fit for duty.'[7]

Despite all the upheaval, the six years of military presence on Tiri had little effect on the island's ecology. Probably more influential would be an increased awareness of Tiri in the minds of people who would guide the island's future path. Also significant for New Zealand as a whole were the widened horizons of the thousands of servicemen and women who had served overseas.

Wartime experience

Some of the people relevant to the Tiri story were active in the war years: Alf King (AHB signalman) was in Signals on Mount Victoria; Tom Clark (later a keeper) was a radio operator on flying boats in Fiji; Graham Turbott (ornithologist) was on Coastal Watch in the Auckland Islands; Brigadier Gilbert (head of World Wildlife Fund in the 1980s) commanded the gun battery at Fort Takapuna, Narrow Neck; Darcy O'Brien (later Crown Commissioner of Lands) was on Fire Command Post on North Head; and the legendary flyer Fred Ladd was an RNZAF officer/pilot. Darcy O'Brien, now in his eighties, knew Des Waite, one of the signalmen who drowned, though, as Mr O'Brien recalled recently, 'he went into the Navy, and I went into the Army'.

~

SIX

MODERNISATION

After the war the military personnel withdrew from Tiri as swiftly as they had arrived, but the buildings lingered, with evidence of the wartime occupation remaining today. Trevor Scott built a cowshed on the foundations of the first PWSS in the 1950s.[1] Concrete foundations of the second PWSS buildings are in the bush in the centre of the island. The FOP building (the Fourth House) was demolished and pushed over the cliff. The concrete FOP tower proved harder to destroy but was finally blown up by the Navy in 1966 and only a concrete base remains today. Unfortunately, in blowing up the tower, the Navy also destroyed a small population of bats, probably the last on Tiri.

When the war ended, Tiri reverted to Auckland Harbour Board administration, and three signalmen returned. Betty Roper, née King, was the youngest daughter of the King family, who now returned to Tiri:

> When the station was to reopen, my father was offered the position of Chief Signalman which he accepted and along with two other ex-Navy men, a Mr Bill Ford and his wife Bobby, and Mr George Chamberlain, his wife Georgina and their two little boys, moved to the island in 1945. On occupying the station he realised that a lot of work was needed to be done and asked for this work to be carried out, as the years of neglect showed its mark on the houses and surrounding station buildings.

Tiri lighthouse station from the north, 1955. The Principal Keeper's House is at far left, with the signal mast and FOP behind the lighthouse. The rudimentary 'airstrip' is at top right. At rear is the Pinnacles rocks where the *Triumph* went aground.
GeoSmart Ltd 37160

Alf King inside the signal tower, 1946.
Dora Walthew, née King

Far right: George Chamberlain and Alf King use the winch to unload the AHB supply ship *Ferro* in 1947.
George Chamberlain

MOT maintenance workers Henry Phillips and Joe Conlon repaint the lighthouse, c.1965.
Peter Taylor

The Kings occupied the Chief Signalman's (Principal Keeper's) House, which was still 'a lovely home'. Betty and the two young Chamberlain boys played at ghosts in the empty PWSS buildings in the centre of the island. On rainy days there were books. 'One of the little sheds near the stables … was turned into a library. … This was a very exciting time for me, helping mother with the extra workload, as well as getting used to the Correspondence School work.'[2]

Later the Lighthouse Service ran a library service. Each supply boat brought a box of books, which was sent on to the next lighthouse by the next boat. A library overdue notice is still in the Tiri files, and the last shipment of books remains on Tiri from when the lighthouse was automated in the 1980s. The eclectic selection of both fiction and non-fiction may go some way to explaining why so many lighthouse keepers have written books.

The wharf had been extended by the time of the Second World War and a winch fitted. Wooden rails guided a cart along the wharf.

But the signalmen, post-war, expected better working conditions. Things came to a head when the AHB proposed reducing their supply boat from weekly to fortnightly, and Betty King's happy lighthouse life ended abruptly: 'In May 1947 we took a

holiday to Auckland and while there we heard that the Harbour Board was thinking of closing the island down. Also, my mother took ill and died suddenly. Father had to return to the island and make necessary arrangements for the closure of its station.'

Responsibility for the lighthouse reverted to the Ministry of Transport (MOT) in 1947 and lighthouse keepers returned to Tiri. The red tower was painted white. (When it was repainted in 1996 this job took 16 days.)

Radio beacon

In 1935 a radio beacon had been installed as a navigation aid for shipping. This gave out a signal that vessels could triangulate with other beacons to determine their position. It was powered by a generator driven off the diesel engines for the diaphonic foghorn. Initially the beacon was turned on at regular stated intervals, but later it was activated only on request from a ship. It was in operation from 1935 to 1957, and shows in photos as a tall, dark mast southwest of the lighthouse, with an aerial extending from it to the lighthouse (see photo on page 51).

Advances in technology continued: in 1955, diesel generators produced electricity to power the light, and the houses were allowed two hours' 'domestic power' a week. Russell Miell and Charles Brazier maintained the lighthouses for the Public Works Department at this time, and brought the keepers' houses up to State Housing specifications. When they turned the generator on in the daytime to do their work, the keepers' wives had electricity for a few more hours. The houses also got a small kerosene fridge that, according to Trevor Scott, a keeper post-war, 'had a mind of its own'.

A rudimentary airstrip was made on the ridge at the southern end of the island in the 1950s, but it was barely used.

Charles Brazier helped build 'The Bach', a small house for relieving keepers, in the 1960s. The builders wrote their names and the date up in the rafters. The Bach is on the eastern side, adjacent to where the Chief Signalman's or Principal Keeper's House stood. Principal Keeper Peter Taylor was cleaning up after the demolition of the old house in the mid-1960s. As related in his entertaining book, *As Darker Grows the Night*, the last item to go was 'a huge concrete meat safe'. He hoisted the heavy load onto the bucket of the tractor and drove slowly forward, stopping well short of the edge of the cliff. But when he lowered the bucket, the tractor began to slide gently forward. He touched the brakes, then moved quickly into reverse gear. 'Too late.' As the front wheels left the ground, Peter stepped off the back. 'It was probably the coolest act of my life.' The tractor bounced down the cliff onto the rocks below 'with an almighty crash'. 'The seagulls became very perturbed, as of course could only be expected when a tractor fell on them from 300 feet.'[3] It was a month before a replacement tractor arrived, and during that time all the supplies had to be brought up from the wharf by wheelbarrow.

The lighthouse stores boat was now another *Stella*, skippered by Rex Brown, while the *Colville* serviced the lighthouses around the Gulf. The Tiri channel, though only four kilometres wide, can be a treacherous piece of water, especially under conditions of 'wind against tide'. Heather Mander describes a frightening trip back from Whangaparaoa about 1960. She and her husband Ray, the principal keeper, had taken their little son Mark across in the island's lifeboat for a doctor's appointment. The forecast had been for settled weather, but halfway back to Tiri a storm blew up from the north and it became very rough:

> Ray told me that if the outboard motor ran out of petrol I was to put Mark in the bottom of the boat and row while he refuelled the motor. [The motor used more fuel in the rough, and the tank may not have held enough.] I looked at all the water we had shipped and said, 'I can't put him in that', but Ray said that if I didn't keep the boat steady we could capsize. Fortunately the motor chugged on and got us safely home again.

As the first centenary of the Tiri lighthouse approached there were rumblings from Aucklanders that the Tiri light was 'just a glimmer. Like someone standing up there with a torch.'[4] Sir Ernest Davis, a former mayor of Auckland, prominent businessman and a keen yachtsman, personally donated £80,000 to give

Tiri lighthouse station, c.1965. In the foreground are the two storage sheds and tractor shed.
Peter Taylor

Fred Ladd

'A shower of spray and we're away.' This was the catchphrase of the legendary Fred Ladd, a pilot with Tourist Air Travel Ltd from 1951 to about 1970, and a valued lifeline. Ladd could take his Widgeon amphibian aircraft almost anywhere — including under the Auckland Harbour Bridge. 'Fred would just land in there, and it wouldn't matter how the weather was.'[5] He was an angel of mercy for any sick or injured person, flying Peter Taylor out after he fell off scaffolding when building the shed. Taylor's injury — a badly broken leg — ended his lighthouse career.[6]

Russell Miell remembers flying with Fred Ladd to Little Barrier: 'He always dropped newspapers off. He dived in over the houses at Tiri and I threw the paper out and it landed in the tree just beside the house.' 'I've always wanted to get one right on the little gallery round the tower,' Ladd told Shirley Maddock, 'but mostly I end up in the cow paddock, or down among the cabbages.'[7]

Ladd scrawled doggerel verse on the newspapers:

> Tiri Islanders in the waves
> Are your eyes like hollow caves
>
> For the dawn has only come
> Yet still no sign of sun.
>
> Wakey Wakey do you hear me yet
> Of course you do I'll bet.[8]

When Ladd took George Harrison up in June 1964, the Beatle composed the verse that day!

Top right: Fred Ladd's amphibian plane on Hobbs Beach. Tiri Archives

Fred Ladd, Mrs Mander and children, c.1960. Trevor Scott

Auckland the light he felt it deserved. Such a generous donation generated much publicity. Peter Taylor was still on the island when the new light, containing a tiny but powerful 1800-watt xenon bulb, was installed.

Unfortunately Sir Ernest had died by the time his Davis Marine Light was first lit on 30 March 1965, just over 100 years after the Tiri lighthouse was first illuminated. Peter Taylor describes the moment when the engineer pressed the switch: 'We gasped. Eight long needles of intense, icy-blue light reached to the horizon in an instant, and swept around like the spokes of

Soon after the announcement of the new Davis light, it seemed to Aucklanders that Tiri's light had got brighter overnight. They were right. When checking the old light in the run-up to installing the new one, the engineers had found that the lenses were badly out of alignment. Generations of keepers, diligently cleaning the lenses, had used the focusing prism as a convenient step. In doing so they had altered the light's angle upwards until it was actually doing a better job of guiding planes than shipping.

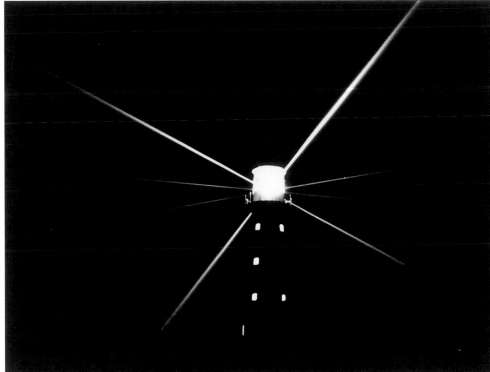

'Eight long needles of light': the Davis Marine Light, 1965. Peter Taylor

Left: Installing the Davis Marine Light in 1965. Peter Taylor

Far left: Peter Taylor holding old and new lighthouse bulbs, 1965. Peter Taylor

a huge cartwheel.'[9] At 11 million cp it was the brightest light in the Southern Hemisphere, visible to the horizon — and beyond. 'As a loom in the sky, it has been reported by ships 50 miles away, and some North Shore residents go to sleep watching it sweeping past their bedroom walls.'[10] It could even, reportedly, be seen by the Apollo astronauts in space.[11]

To power the Davis light, the island was connected to the national grid in 1967 via an underwater power cable. Laying the cable had required meticulous planning but it went without a hitch.

But 'the Sir Ernest Davis light on Tiri was of doubtful benefit to us mariners,' comments Frank Arnott. 'It ... dominated the whole Gulf at night' and affected the night vision of sailors, preventing them from seeing other navigational lights about the Gulf.[12] 'The xenon bulbs ... lasted 100 hours and cost $600 to replace. When the xenon light was lit, the operator had to wear a welding mask to avoid eye damage.'[13] And when a bulb exploded it shattered the lighthouse's lenses. Less than 20 years after it first

Lighthouse facts

Tiritiri Matangi Island is the oldest lighthouse still in operation in New Zealand. The collection of buildings — the light, the signal tower, the two keepers' houses, and surrounding buildings — is the best-preserved compound in New Zealand, and the only one open to the public. The lighthouse, a Category 1 Registered Historic Place, is now administered by the Maritime Safety Authority, a part of MOT, but the remaining buildings are the responsibility of the Department of Conservation.

Situated at Latitude 36°36' South, Longitude 174°54' East, the tower stands 21 metres high and is 4.7 metres in diameter at the base. The light itself is 91 metres above sea level and can be seen for 18 nautical miles (33 kilometres) in standard weather conditions. It flashes once every 15 seconds.

dazzled the Gulf, the Davis Marine Light was replaced in 1984 by a far less powerful quartz iodine light (1.6 million cp). The lighthouse was partially automated and 'de-manned' at this time. Ray Walter, the last lighthouse keeper on Tiritiri Matangi, was able to stay on to run the revegetation project.

'Then ... someone put an anchor through the power cable. ... It was a fishing vessel what did that.'[14] Alarms sounded on Tiri and Ray Walter had to start the auxiliary generator to keep the light going. After the third cable failure in 1989, the island was removed from the national grid, and electricity was supplied by diesel generator again.

In 1991, the light was converted to batteries charged by solar panels, and so it remains today. From 1990 to 2002 the light was a faint 300,000 cp from a 60-watt bulb that had previously been the Davis light's emergency light. An upgrade in 2002 increased it to 1.2 million cp. The present Tiri light is a New Zealand-built power-beam light.

The lantern at night, 1995.
Pat Greenfield

Facing page: Tiri lighthouse station, 1992.
Pat Greenfield

~

SEVEN

THE DAWN CHORUS

'A visitor has only to visit one of the well-bushed off-shore islands to realise something of the richness of the birdlife, exemplified in one curious way by the 1600-kilometre overlap of parrots and penguins.' – R. B. Sibson[1]

With its predator-free status (apart from the kiore), Tiri has always had a good variety of birds, of both native and exotic species. This was so even when farming had reduced the natural bush to only a few pockets in the valleys. Neil Mitchell recalls the bush being filled with birdsong even before any restoration started. This chapter looks at the 'common' birds that are found naturally on Tiri.

All native birds are protected, as are any that arrive from overseas under their own steam. These are usually blown here from Australia in strong westerly winds. The immigrants include silvereyes, which arrived 150 years ago, and the welcome swallow (1958).[2] The spur-winged plover, which has only recently reached the Auckland area, first bred on Tiri in 1996. Much earlier, ancestors of the takahe and pukeko had also come from Australia.

Other 'Aussies' originated from caged birds. The kookaburra, galah and sulphur-crested cockatoo have been occasional visitors to Tiri – even a frightened budgie appeared in the bunkhouse once. Rosellas nest on the island, and a pair of magpies are tolerated because Ray Walter feels they control mynas. One unwelcome parrot, which has not (yet) reached Tiri, is the rainbow lorikeet, which is a threat to native species such as the tui. DOC found many lorikeets on Whangaparaoa Peninsula during their eradication attempts.

The numbers of Australasian quail exploded after the kiore eradication, some pairs having 12 chicks per clutch. Visitors sometimes mistake their dumpy brown shape for a kiwi or even a rat! Up close, the drab bird reveals complex feather markings in pleasing patterns of browns and greys. On the track, where they enjoy a dust bath, they may walk right past a stationary observer. If flushed, they rise up from the undergrowth with a startling whirr of their stubby wings. The bumblebee-sized chicks are so tiny that every dried leaf presents an obstacle in their path.

By 1870 numerous exotic bird species had been introduced to Auckland, including the blackbird, sparrow and myna.[3] Since most pose little threat to the native birds, no effort is made to reduce their numbers on Tiri, except for mynas, which threatened saddlebacks initially. Thousands of starlings fly over from Whangaparaoa to roost on Tiri each night, and skylarks rise, singing their liquid song over the mown meadow on Coronary Hill.

Tui feeding on kowhai blossom.

Roving Tortoise Photos

Left: This charming study of an Australasian quail was a winner in the 2000 Supporters' photo competition.

Val Smytheman

Facing page: Male bellbird.

Alex Mitchell

59

Puriri flowers and berries are available all year round. Val Smytheman

Right: A tui capped with orange flax pollen. Max McRae

The first bird notes on Tiri were made during the lighthouse construction, and the keeper, Anders Hansen, made careful observations. R. B. (Dick) Sibson, the well-known ornithologist, visited Tiri in 1945–46. His list of 27 species included the redpoll and pipit, both of which are absent today. Chukor were also introduced but failed to become established.

When Alan Esler was reporting on Tiri's vegetation for the Hauraki Gulf Marine Park Board in 1970, his son Lloyd, still a schoolboy, conducted a bird survey and found 25 species. The Ornithological Society, which recorded 31 species in 1969, started regular twice-yearly counts in 1987. By 1989, 39 breeding species of birds were recorded, with an additional 11 species visiting the island, and by 1994 the number had risen to 76.[4] This book records 84 bird species sighted on or near Tiritiri Matangi, including the 11 species that have been translocated.

Bellbirds and tui have always been present, though in pitifully reduced numbers by the end of the farming era: in 1969, the Ornithological Society counted *every individual* — 24 bellbirds and 21 tui. Tiri then had the closest population of bellbirds to the Auckland area, where they had been extinct since the 1860s.[4] When John Craig arrived in 1974, he realised that for part of the year the bellbirds were utterly dependent on the fruit and flowers of the two surviving puriri trees and he started supplementary feeding with sugar water to help the birds. Bellbirds enjoy the nectar from wattle flowers (*Albizzia*), and in springtime Wattle Valley rings with the song of bellbird choirs.

Endemic, native or exotic?

Endemic species are those which occur only in New Zealand, for example the stitchbird. **Native** species occur here naturally but are also found elsewhere, for example the fantail, which is also native to Australia and some islands. **Exotic** species have been introduced by humans, for example the myna.

The supplementary feeding stations set up for the stitchbirds in 1995 were designed to exclude bellbirds, which by that time had sufficient natural food on the island. But when, in 1998, one bellbird learned how to get in, the rest quickly followed. The sound of competing birds around a feeder can be deafening. Tui are too big to fit through the mesh: one enterprising tui did once find its way inside a feeder, but it needed assistance to get out again. The red plastic sugar dispensers are hummingbird feeders (specially imported from the USA), which help to keep the sugar solution clean.

In the spring, bellbirds and tui feast on nectar from the golden kowhai flowers, transferring their allegiance to flax as the tall stems come into flower around breeding time. Suddenly, new birds are spotted on Tiri — orange-headed bellbirds and tui, capped by the abundant flax pollen. In the years when kakariki ate most of the flax flowers, this important food source of flax nectar was denied to the honeyeaters, whose breeding suffered as a result.

New Zealand pigeon (kereru). Peter Craw

Drought reduces the food available to the birds. Stitchbird nests failed in the hot, dry summer of 1998 when fruit didn't mature. In hot weather the island's streams dwindle to a trickle, and birds throng to the water troughs — which were actually built for birds to drink at, not to bathe in as they do now. (The seats at two of these troughs were also built to give pleasant views down a valley, but these are now obscured by trees.)

When food is scarce, tui fly to the mainland, with birds banded on Tiri having been seen as far away as Birkenhead on Auckland's North Shore. Bellbirds rarely fly across the Tiri channel, but a few birds have been breeding in Shakespear Regional Park on Whangaparaoa since 1993.

Aggressively territorial, the powerful tui will dive-bomb other birds, striking them in the back of the neck with its sharp beak — a kokako is believed to have been killed this way. Noisy aerial battles between tui neighbours often enliven the bush. Tui song is a rich tumble of sound, incorporating clear bell-like whistles, interspersed with the harsh croaks that distinguish the tui's from the bellbird's more mellifluous song. Some of the notes are in the ultrasonic spectrum — which accounts for those frustrating moments when a bird is clearly singing its heart out but we mortals can't hear a thing! Some tui have learned to imitate kokako on Tiri, fooling some guides until they hear the characteristic tui croak.

The clear, repeated call of the kingfisher carries through the bush. Despite their name, kingfishers on Tiri eat insects, skinks and even crabs, leaving the crab shells on Hobbs Beach. Their nesting hole is made by the adult birds flying straight at a clay bank until a foothold is attained, so it is not surprising that a pair will use the same hole each year. One pair nests in the bank near the wharf, and while Ray Walter is giving his introductory talk, a parent bird may be waiting on the wharf railing with a skink dangling from its mouth. Kingfisher holes can be seen up among the roots of the big pohutukawa on Hobbs Beach.

Kereru are on the increase on Tiri. These huge pigeons sit silently on a branch overhead, although the flash of their white bibs may give them away. As the only surviving bird large enough to eat the fruit of trees such as karaka and taraire, they are an essential part of seed distribution in a mature New Zealand forest.

Kaka, which can fly long distances, visit regularly — sometimes for weeks on end — but have not yet nested on Tiri. In the 1990s two big nesting boxes were put up for kaka. A pair arrived, made an inspection, and left. Vic Hunter, who built the boxes, felt like handing out a questionnaire on their failings.

Spine-tailed swifts are occasionally sighted. Welcome swallows are common. A pair decided the new toilet-roll holders at the landing toilets were the ideal place to build a nest. Each day Barbara Walter removed the nest beginnings, but the birds promptly rebuilt. Finally she placed a rock on each holder, and was severely scolded by the swallows for doing so.

A caution from Ray Walter

Bird whistles, lure tapes etc should not be used on Tiri. Similarly, people should not overdo using sounds to attract birds, such as the stone-tapping for fern birds, or war-whooping for petrels. These disturb the birds and can upset their breeding patterns.

Below right: Daphne, the tame paradise shelduck.
Julia Sich

Below: Shining cuckoo (photo not taken on Tiri).
Geoff Moon

Often it is the oddities that catch the attention: a cock pheasant, sulphur-crested cockatoos in the 1950s, the pied blackbird, the white bellbird, the lone white goose (Goosey Nomates), and Daphne, the tame paradise shelduck who arrived in August 2003 and stayed. She patrols the lighthouse area, terrorising small children, and flies down to the wharf to farewell visitors. Paradise shelducks are grazing ducks. They frequently breed on Tiri, but are careless parents, losing their ducklings by attrition.

Spotless crakes are more often heard than seen. These tiny, dark-coloured rails, like miniature weka, were very common when the grass was long on Tiri. When Ray Walter mowed in a spiral he found he herded them into the centre, so he mowed from the centre out. He once found a spotless crake dead on the lighthouse gantry. Crakes can be heard, and sometimes seen, near the bunkhouse dam, and on the Wattle Track at the 'Crakeless Spot' — so-called because no one but Morag Fordham, a long-time supporter and knowledgeable birder, ever sees a crake there. One day, to the envy of all unsuccessful crake-spotters, she reported rescuing a baby crake whose foot was entangled in the mesh of the boardwalk. However, on the wharf dam, these normally shy and retiring birds are very visible, walking a regular circuit at the water's edge. In fact, Chris Gaskin of Kiwi Wildlife Tours says that Tiri is the best place in New Zealand to see the spotless crake.

One lone weka has been resident for over 17 years. No one knows whence it came, though a boatie may have dropped it off

Cuckoo

Cuckoos are brood parasites, laying their egg in another species' nest and leaving the host parents to raise the chick. Two species of cuckoos breed in New Zealand. Both are found on Tiri, but only one breeds there at present.

The Shining Cuckoo, *Chrysococcyx lucidus*, returns to New Zealand from the Solomon Islands in October. Its song, a harbinger of spring, is a repeated rising call, with falling notes at the end. The mid-sized bird is rarely seen. It is a vivid iridescent green, its barred breast shimmering as it catches the light. The shining cuckoo lays one egg in the nest of the grey warbler, which is a smaller bird. The warbler parents incubate the cuckoo egg along with their own, but after the cuckoo chick hatches it evicts the warblers' own eggs and young, thus ensuring the little parents devote all their energy to feeding the 'cuckoo in the nest'. Grey warblers were seen feeding a shining cuckoo chick on Tiri in spring 2000.

The Long-Tailed Cuckoo, *Eudynamys taitensis*, winters in the Solomon Islands and in Eastern Polynesia. It lays its eggs in whitehead nests in the North Island, while in the South Island it parasitises yellowhead and brown creeper nests. There is a great size differential, the whitehead being only 16 centimetres long, while the cuckoo is 40 centimetres, though much of this is its long tail. Although whiteheads have been on Tiri for over 10 years, and long-tailed cuckoos have been occasionally sighted or heard — the call is a harsh shriek, sometimes heard at night — there is no evidence yet of them breeding on Tiri. This is partly because these cuckoos usually return to the place where they hatched. They were seen more frequently in the 1970s than they are now. However, with the whitehead now the most abundant bird on Tiri it is only a matter of time before the cuckoo follows.

bird is apologising for its temerity in singing.

Not every native bird is mentioned here: the 11 bird species that have been introduced to Tiri each have their own box inserted in the text. These are on the following pages:

Translocated Species	Approx no. on Tiri 2004	Page no.
Kakariki (red-crowned parakeet)	Several hundred	69
North Island saddleback	Several hundred	87
Brown teal	25–30 approximately	90
Whitehead	1000 approximately	93
Takahe	18	127
North Island robin	189	98
Little spotted kiwi	50–60	97
Stitchbird (hihi)	188	122
North Island kokako	15	133
Fernbird	25–30	110
North Island tomtit	32	134
Tuatara *(not a bird, of course)*	60	107

Pukeko nest communally.
John Craig

Left: Pukeko. Peter Craw

Below: Spotless crake.
Peter Craw

from Kawau Island, as also happened on Waiheke Island a while back. It is sometimes heard calling and does a good imitation of a kiwi. Weka attack chicks and eggs and can be aggressive to people, so this one must remain solitary. There are no banded rails on Tiri and they are not wanted for the same reasons.

Pukeko, the slimmer cousins of the takahe, need no introduction. They stalk proudly around flicking their white scuts, but rush off shrieking if anyone gets too close. They live in family groups and are excellent parents, especially in comparison to the takahe. Though pukeko can fly, they usually prefer to climb to a high viewpoint, like a muehlenbeckia mound. They compete to some extent with takahe and in a standoff it is often the larger takahe that retreats first.

Perky little tomtits have visited occasionally — probably from Little Barrier Island, and these friendly birds were the most recent species to be introduced to Tiri, in April 2004.

One of the sweetest songs is that of the grey warbler, a tiny morsel of a bird that is merely glimpsed as it flicks across the track. It sings a long tune, sweet and tremulous, as though the

Bird names

For many birds the Maori name is taking precedence over the English one. Thus *kereru* is preferred to *pigeon* and, on Tiri, *hihi* is used equally with *stitchbird*. Some names remain English — it is usually a *fantail*, not a *piwakawaka*, but this may change in future. In general this book uses the name that is commonly used on Tiri at the time of writing.

The Maori plural is the same as the singular: thus it is one takahe and three pukeko.

Morepork. Matt Low

Pied shag. Peter Craw

BIRD PREDATORS

Bird predators on Tiri pose a novel problem because their diet comprises, of necessity, mostly endangered birds. In morepork nests, regurgitated leg bands, and even an intact banded leg, show that the adults and their chicks consume stitchbirds, robins and saddlebacks.

A morepork was seen hiding under the Kawerau Track boardwalk in 2003. It caught a saddleback in broad daylight and took it up to the nest to feed to its three chicks. A racket of bird alarm calls greeted a school group on the Wattle Track, also in 2003. They found a morepork sitting on a branch over the track being mobbed by a hysterical, whirling group of bellbirds and others. Moreporks sometimes nest and roost in the crown of a ponga and this is a good place to look for them.

Australasian harriers have developed a taste for kokako chicks, and also take brown teal ducklings. When kiore numbers were at their highest in the 1970s, up to 24 harriers could be seen hunting over Tiri at one time. Nowadays, only one or two visit occasionally. In 2002 conservation officers were authorised to shoot harriers, a decision that engendered lively debate in the *Dawn Chorus,* the Supporters' newsletter. A similar problem arose in 2003 with the immediate predation of three of seven newly introduced brown teal and again shooting was authorised, but only one hawk was ever shot.

SHOREBIRDS

Many shorebirds nest on Tiri. The large colonies of gulls and terns on the eastern rocks can be viewed from near The Bach. White-fronted terns gather in flocks on the wharf railings, and are sometimes seen flying eastwards across the island with sprats in their beaks to feed their chicks. Oystercatchers nest south of the wharf, and a family can sometimes be observed, slowly working the shoreline. The endangered New Zealand dotterel and the Caspian tern nest on the rocks off Hobbs Beach.

A large roost of about 60 spotted shags was discovered in 1992 on a cliff south of the lighthouse. This is their northern-most recorded roost site. That year, too, Bird Rescue released 11 spotted shags on Tiri.

Anders Hansen: The first conservationist

Anders Hansen writes: 'The little black shag of which I sent some eggs, is, I think, a new arrival here. I feel sure they did not nest here last year. It appears that the tree shags can only have been building on the island the last few years as only one or two trees were occupied. This year new trees have been built in, and it is on these new trees that the small shag has built its nests. The trees in which the shags build are very soon killed by the acrid nature of the excrement.

'I think the reason of the recent appearance of tree-building shags here is due to the fact that the rabbits which at one time overran the island are now all died out.

'When rabbits were plentiful, parties of shooters came down here and the shags offered admirable targets for their abominable pea-rifles. Only a short time ago some young man came here to shoot shags, telling me that he would get sixpence per pair of legs, or some such sum. I told him that even if it was desirable to shoot the shags, I thought it would be very inhuman to do so with the helpless young chicks in the nests to be left to die of starvation, and further, pointed out to him that the shags building here, so far as I knew, lived exclusively on seafish of which there was an abundance for all. Any how so long as I am in charge of Tiri there will be no shooting of birds except that they be wanted for scientific purposes.'[5]

Tiritiri Lighthouse
16 Oct 1907
Dear Sir

I have been around the Island twice to see if it were possible to locate nest of the blue crane — have not succeeded although the birds are always about. There are so many caves on the eastern side in which they can make their nest.
I remain
Sir
Yours faithfully
A. Hansen.

Since Hansen's day the reef heron, as the blue crane is now more commonly known, has had to compete with the white-faced heron, which arrived from Australia and started breeding in 1941. Both are seen on Tiri, though the reef heron less so than before.

Tiritiri Lighthouse
16 Oct 1907

I notice that the Terns are beginning to congregate on the rocks so it won't be long before they begin nesting.
Hansen

SEABIRDS

On Little Wooded Island fluttering shearwaters and common diving petrels nest in great numbers. Approximately 15,000 pairs nest in an area of less than one hectare, giving a density of two to three pairs per square metre. The grey-faced petrel nests at the 'Petrel Station' on the cliffs above Hobbs Beach. The ground here is very unstable and people must not venture off the track. Mel Galbraith, who has studied the petrels for years, has found one bird aged over 40, and another aged 39.

Little blue penguins can be seen from the ferry, bobbing about like buoyant bottles. They come ashore at night, climbing up as far as the lighthouse to sleep and nest. For much of the

White-fronted terns like the wharf. Margaret Chappell

Left: Variable oystercatchers work the shoreline. Alex Mitchell

The Galbraith children inspecting the penguin boxes in 1989.
Mel Galbraith

Below: Graham Jones studying a penguin, 1975.
University of Auckland

Below right: Little blue penguin. Peter Craw

year, penguins can be seen in the penguin boxes near the wharf. These were designed by John Craig and built by John McLeod. Graham Jones, the first graduate student to study penguins on Tiri, wrote in 1990: 'The penguin nest boxes … near the jetty have finally won approval from their intended tenants, the little blue penguins. Having decided that this might be a reasonable sort of place to raise a family, they have hatched their first chicks this season. This is good news for visitors to Tiri who can now view the private life of the penguin without causing too much disturbance, simply by lifting the lid and peering through the glass.'

After raising their young, the adults return to the island to moult. During this time they cannot go to sea because their plumage is not waterproof. Unfortunately a safe shelter cannot protect a bird against every misfortune: during spring storms in 2003, all the penguin chicks in the nesting boxes starved when their parents could not catch enough food for them.

EIGHT

GERMINATION

The 1960s and 1970s were a time of growing ecological awareness worldwide, with Rachel Carson's 1962 book *Silent Spring* sounding the first warnings about insecticides in the environment. New Zealand had embraced DDT with the same enthusiasm as the rest of the world, and with a similar ignorance of its dangers. Bob Drey, a senior planning officer at Lands and Survey, recalls Wildlife Service officers, wearing no protective clothing, mixing chemicals 'by the bucket load'.

Responsibility for New Zealand's environment was fragmented at this time: the Lands and Survey Department administered National Parks and Public Reserves, subject to the Reserves Act; the Wildlife Service, which administered the Wildlife Act, was responsible for protected birds and game birds; and the Forest Service was responsible for State Forests — and this included milling the trees where appropriate. Rivalry between the three departments sometimes impeded progress.

The Hauraki Gulf Maritime Park was established in 1967 to protect some of the islands of the Gulf (others were privately owned). It was administered by a government-appointed board with the Commissioner of Crown Lands (CCL), Darcy O'Brien, as *ex officio* chairman. The board was responsible for the day-to-day administration of the park, and much was achieved thanks to the vision of the board members, whose services were voluntary. People were encouraged to become involved in park activities and 'Friends of the Gulf' received a chatty and informative quarterly newsletter.

Tiritiri Matangi Island was and is Crown land. Since 1841 it

had been a lighthouse reserve, with the majority of the island being leased for farming. In 1970, the Marine Department, deciding it only needed 'a bit for the light, and a bit for a cow', returned the remainder to the Crown. Rather than sell the island off, as might happen in today's market, the Department of Lands and Survey in the person of CCL Darcy O'Brien gazetted it as a recreation island, with 14 hectares remaining as lighthouse reserve. Tiri was added to the HGMP (whose chairman admits that his dual role probably blurred the lines of decision-making a bit). The island was familiar to most of the board members from boating trips. An HGMP leaflet of the time, with the text 'It's your island … ', shows photos of rolling farmland and people enjoying the beach. There were two classifications of reserves:

The ideal board meeting: the Hauraki Gulf Maritime Park Board inspecting Little Barrier Island in December 1971. L to R: John Seabrook, Harold Watts, Jack Lovell, Darcy O'Brien, Ted Lees, Jim Holdaway and Arnold Baldwin. Ted Lees

Jack Hobbs demolishes his bach, c.1971, leaving the woolshed, which was later used as accommodation by the university researchers.
Daisy Burrell

'The '60s and '70s were a time of frantic efforts to save several bird species from extinction,' writes Don Merton, who was the first New Zealand Wildlife Service's protected fauna officer, based in Auckland from 1962 to 1967. These efforts included Merton's successful transfers of the North Island saddleback from Hen Island to other offshore islands in the Hauraki Gulf. Wally Sander, the chief ranger for Lands and Survey, recalls that he, Don Merton, Dick Veitch and other Wildlife Service people discussed the future of Tiritiri Matangi as they passed the island in the 1970s.

John Craig, a newly appointed junior lecturer in zoology at the University of Auckland, was searching for a research project. Reading in the newspaper about the 1974 kakariki transfer, he arranged to visit Tiri. He remembers walking up from Fishermans Bay through rank grass. It was 'really, really hard walking'. As an ecologist he was keen to work on something other than birds, and on Tiri he found not only tui, bellbirds and pukeko but also kiore. The HGMP Board was happy to allow research on Tiri, and thus began Craig's long association with the island.

Craig and his students visited Tiri monthly, either travelling on the lighthouse tender, *Stella*, or coming over from Whangaparaoa in a 14-foot aluminium Parker craft, dubbed *The Tin Coffin*, and skippered at speed by Murray Douglas. In a small, open boat, loaded down with people and equipment, it was only safe to cross in calm weather, and on one occasion the passengers mutinied, insisting on turning back.

They stayed in the disused woolshed on the beach, which was pretty disreputable, but 'fun!' The bunks were constructed from flotsam and jetsam picked up off the beaches. Botany lecturer Neil Mitchell, newly arrived from England, was enchanted to find that the sea lapped the foundations at high tide, and he could fish for his dinner from the veranda. However, having a kiore run over his face in the night was not so enchanting. Feeling the need for a botanist's input on Tiri, Craig had approached Mitchell in 1978. The strong partnership of two

recreation and scientific, but there was little on Tiri's bare slopes to attract the scientist.

The board consulted the DSIR botanist Alan Esler, who spent a week on Tiri in 1970.[1] Describing the depleted state of forest remnants, the remaining pohutukawa on the cliffs and the effects of cattle browse even in the dense forest, Esler concluded, 'It is clear that the forest would clothe most of the island quite rapidly in the absence of sheep and cattle. Replanting would be quite unnecessary … natural reafforestation should be considered. … A century hence, there would be little evidence to show that Tiritiri was once one of the bald islands of the Hauraki Gulf.'[2]

On the basis of Esler's report, Darcy O'Brien (wearing his 'Commissioner of Crown Lands' hat) decided not to renew the farming lease. Prophetically, Hobbs told O'Brien that if the stock were taken off, the island would merely come away in short scrub and he doubted very much if native bush would find its way through the scrub.

dissimilar but complementary personalities continues today.

Neil Mitchell describes the magic of setting off from Whangaparaoa on a mirror-calm sea and arriving at a deserted Tiri soon after dawn. Drifting quietly in, they were greeted then, as now, by bellbird song. He also remembers his pleasure on entering the dense green forest of Bush 1 (the Kawerau Track) with, again, abundant birdsong — even back then.

But the lighthouse keeper, Tom Clark, mistrusted students and their 'hippy' ways, a sentiment shared by the HGMP chief ranger, George 'Shorty' Holmes. Clark offered no help, even though the students had to carry heavy equipment from the wharf to Hobbs Beach. There were allegations of 'sex and drug orgies', with a relieving keeper warning John Craig that a police launch was on its way to search them for drugs. Craig feels part

Kakariki

Red-crowned parakeet, kakariki
Cyanoramphus novaezelandiae novaezelandiae
Protected native

The kakariki was the first bird to be reintroduced to Tiri. In 1973, Dick Veitch, the Wildlife Service's protected fauna officer for Auckland, got permission to release kakariki on both Tiritiri Matangi and Cuvier Islands. In January 1974, about 30 cage-reared birds were flown up from Mount Bruce National Wildlife Centre to Ardmore Airport, South Auckland. Chris Smuts-Kennedy, the fauna

conservation officer for the Wildlife Service in Whangarei, collected them from the airport and drove them to Whitianga but, finding that the boat booked to take them to Cuvier was not there, he had no option but to drive the birds back to Auckland, by which time some of them were dying from stress in the January heat. He put the surviving birds into a friend's aviary for a few days to recover and then, aided by Wally Sander, released them on Tiri. 'It was the first time in the world that captive-reared birds had been successfully released into the wild.'[3] These facts have somehow metamorphosed into a romantic and oft-told tale of the Cuvier-bound kakariki being on a boat that was forced to shelter in the lee of Tiri during a storm. 'Three days later, the weather had not improved. The birds in their cages were becoming distressed, and, fearing they might die, the scientists decided to open the cages and release them on Tiri.'[4] Unfortunately, this version is completely untrue.

More kakariki from Mount Bruce were released on Tiri in the 1970s by John Craig

and Mark Dawe of the University of Auckland. The population remained at low numbers until the kiore eradication in 1993, after which numbers burgeoned.

The well-camouflaged green parrots are usually seen on flax-flower stems, on cabbage trees or feeding on the roadside. They use the tracks as flyways, skimming over people's heads as they zoom past. Kakariki sometimes nest in disused saddleback boxes, or in clumps of muehlenbeckia.

Above: Kakariki are often seen on the ground.
Eve Manning

Left: The blue wings of the kakariki are usually only seen in flight. Peter Craw

A bald island: the university hut in Bush 3 and surrounding landscape, 1978.
Carol West

of the problem was the odd hours that researchers keep. They might have been up all night, if their study subject was nocturnal, but to outside observers they were only seen lounging around on the beach all day 'doing nothing'.

'[Kakariki] liberated on Tiri had been observed in continually decreasing numbers throughout the year,' wrote Dick Veitch in 1975. There were allegations that Tom Clark was catching and selling the attractive green parrots and the HGMP Board asked John Craig to investigate. The university group was reluctant to police the situation, but their hand was forced when they were conducting a census of the birds by playing taped calls and a kakariki responded from inside Clark's house! The keeper was reprimanded by the HGMP Board for what was a breach of the Wildlife Act. He retaliated by arranging with George Holmes for the university's accommodation, the woolshed, to be 'condemned', and it was pulled down in 1978.

The university group then erected an old prefab classroom in Bush 3 above Hobbs Beach. It wasn't a great improvement on the woolshed, having bunks again built from driftwood and an ancient coal range. Electricity came from a 12-volt battery and water came from the roof — Neil Mitchell was often ill from the Tiri water. The chief ranger was ordered to 'produce' the site for the hut, including blasting out a long-drop toilet. He dug the hole 3 feet by 6 feet as John Craig had requested, but made the longer dimension horizontal rather than vertical so it was a very 'short' drop.

To soften the open terrain around the hut the researchers transplanted trees, which 'grew like mad', and they observed how quickly seedlings grew from the droppings of birds perched on the guttering.

The university team wondered: with the growing interest in conservation, more people wanted to visit protected sanctuaries like Little Barrier Island. Could Tiri take some of the pressure off Little Barrier?

But little regeneration was occurring even after eight years. There was some encroachment into the grassed areas from the remnant forest in the valleys: pohutukawa, in particular, were appearing, but bracken was spreading, the grass had become impenetrable and the population of kiore had snowballed. Perhaps the regeneration needed help?

Carol West, Neil Mitchell's first graduate student, demonstrated that the dense grass and bracken prevented the growth of seedlings and any that did grow were devoured by kiore. Her conclusion, that it would take 100 years for Tiri's forest to regenerate, supported Craig's and Mitchell's proposal that the island should be replanted.

It took much persuasion before this novel concept was accepted. The HGMP Board was supportive, but some people in Forest and Bird and the Wildlife Service were negative, one recommending that 'a study period of eight years should be allowed before you interfere with nature'.[5] Paul Green, the chief ranger for the HGMP from 1980 to 1992, helped promote the

University students and their 'hippy' ways: Marjorie Cutting and Colin MacDonald, 1981.
Shona Myers

Tiri replanting idea. He describes the Wildlife Service as 'less than supportive' and thinks they felt threatened by the 'refreshing plan'.

In recognition of the university's work, Tiri was reclassified as a scientific reserve in 1980. The HGMP gave the university the option of excluding the public, but Craig and Mitchell had other plans. Not only were they proposing to replant the island, they also wanted to create an 'Open Sanctuary', a place where endangered birds could be safe, and where the public could view the birds — somewhere, as Craig puts it, for the people of Auckland to see conservation in action. They felt that conservation had become a vicarious experience, something encountered only on TV, or when Aucklanders were asked to put their hands in their pockets to pay for another conservation rescue in the South Island. Tiri, on the other hand, was on their very doorstep.

Ideas similar to this had been put forward a decade earlier by Sander, Merton, Veitch *et al*, and there has been intense and sometimes rancorous debate on who first had the 'bright idea' that resulted in Tiri as it is today. While Tiri may have been on the right path earlier, it was John Craig and Neil Mitchell who instigated the reafforestation project, the introduction of rare birds and the emphasis on Tiri being an *open* sanctuary.

'Now we have to make it work.'

– Don Merton

Ronald Lockley is credited with coining the intriguing oxymoron 'open sanctuary' to describe Tiri.

Curiously, one element that gave such vitality to the project — the huge involvement of the public in the planting process — came about by accident. (See Chapter 10, 'The Spade Brigade'.)

At a time when rare and endangered species were commonly locked away in sanctuaries like Little Barrier, with little or no public access, the open sanctuary concept attracted as much derision as the reafforestation proposal, with detractors insisting that 'rare species and the public don't mix'. But Craig, in particular, persisted, writing endless letters and pounding on many desks until the plan was accepted.

When Tom Clark retired as lighthouse keeper, the man next in line for the coveted posting on Tiri was Ray Walter, a career lighthouse keeper, who, with his wife Val and their family, had been manning the Moko Hinau light for seven years — a long time on such an isolated outpost. Ray Walter's reward was Tiritiri Matangi.

The Moko Hinau lighthouse was to be automated, and the Ministry of Transport (MOT) intended torching the houses. Ray Walter worked to salvage what he could ahead of the flames. Television New Zealand, invited along by the MOT to film the automation of the lighthouse, instead filmed Ray running out of his burning home with doors and fittings. The bath in the upper house on Tiri came from Moko Hinau.[6]

When he arrived on Tiri in 1980, Ray Walter thought the way the university people had been treated was 'diabolical' and he set about making their life easier, transporting their equipment on the tractor, and mowing tracks so they could move around more easily. One who benefited from the university presence was 15-year-old Lynda Walter, who was schooled by correspondence. She enjoyed the company of students only a few years her senior, and with their encouragement went on to graduate masters in anthropology in 1988.

Everyone was conscious that growing and planting an island full of trees would be a costly business. Fortunately the World Wildlife Fund (now simply WWF) was looking for a worthwhile project. WWF's first chairman was Sir Peter Scott, the noted British artist and naturalist whose friend Ronald Lockley had moved to New Zealand (Lockley was instrumental in establishing Miranda Naturalists Trust). In 1982 Lockley and Jim Holdaway took Sir Peter to see Tiri. With them, on Stephen Fisher's classic yacht the MY *Bondi Belle,* went John Craig, Neil Mitchell and Graham Turbott, the noted ornithologist and Emeritus Director of the Auckland War Memorial Museum. WWF took on Tiri as a special project. The New Zealand head of WWF, Brigadier Sir William Gilbert, had been Darcy O'Brien's former commanding officer and he now enlisted O'Brien to help WWF raise funds for the Tiri project. They raised $40,000, much by direct donation and by the sale of a limited-edition bronze tuatara, sculpted by Brian Moore. Since the government of the day matched grants two for one, this gave Tiri a 'seed' fund of $120,000 — a remarkable sum in 1982.

Bob Drey worked with John Craig and Neil Mitchell to draw up a management plan. They produced a simple, straightforward document, giving a blueprint 'to manage Tiritiri as a suitable habitat for some of our rarer and endangered fauna and flora, where people, especially Aucklanders, can view them'.[7] The HGMP Board set up a special management subcommittee, chaired by Graham Turbott, to supervise the Tiri project. Turbott, a most respected scientist, was revered as the father figure of the project. The committee met quarterly on Tiri.

Tiritiri Matangi Island Management Committee

First meeting: 20 July 1983

E. G. Turbott, Chair
J. D. O'Brien, WWF
C. R. Veitch, Wildlife Service
J. L. Craig, Auckland University
N. D. Mitchell, Auckland University
In attendance:
R. Mossman, Chief Ranger
M. Cole, Revegetation Manager
R. Drey, Planning Officer

Discussion: Tree planting programme, rats, saddlebacks, signs, visitor accommodation, new wharf. [8]

Ray Walter, at that time still the lighthouse keeper, also attended the meetings.

Mel Galbraith, a former biology teacher at Glenfield College, recalls Tiri from his own childhood in the 1950s as always being an island on the horizon — a place too remote to visit. He first went there in May 1983, during a symposium run by Craig and Mitchell. He found himself sitting on the grass by the lighthouse beside Sir Charles Fleming, the noted geologist, ornithologist and conservationist, as they listened to the plans for the island's development. Mel felt it was such a big vision that he didn't think anyone could cope with it.

But now misfortune and tragedy struck Ray Walter and his family. Firstly, they learned that the Tiri light was to be automated earlier than planned: by 1984, Ray would be out of a job. Then, his wife Val was diagnosed with cancer and died suddenly. These were cruel blows, especially after the stress of the family's Moko Hinau experience. Lynda Walter recalls 'a terrible sense of sadness and some fear about our future' and how afraid she was for her father at this time. Neil Mitchell spent many hours talking with Ray.

At this black period in Ray's life, hope and salvation came from an unexpected quarter. The Tiri project needed a supervisor. It was hard to find people who liked living on islands. Ray Walter, a lighthouse keeper all his life, was ideal in this respect. Also, Ray had previously applied for the ranger's job on Little Barrier Island; he had shown an interest in the university work

The guardian of Tiri: Ray Walter in 2004.
Margaret Chappell

and become friends with Craig and Mitchell. Though untrained in plantsmanship, he had been growing his own food on lighthouse stations for 20 years, and Neil Mitchell assured him that if he could grow cabbages he could grow trees. Above all, he was — and is — a highly intelligent, articulate, practical man who could turn his hand to almost anything: 'the quintessential Kiwi' as Bob Drey calls him.

It was decided that Ray Walter would progressively transfer from MOT to Lands and Survey over three years. He took over sole charge on Tiri in 1985, the project giving him a new focus and the resilience to overcome his misfortunes. He is still there today, 20 years later.

In 2003, Lady Philippa Scott emailed from Slimbridge, recalling her 1982 visit with pleasure and quoting from her late husband's diary that it had been 'a memorable day'. She also asked if tuatara were now on the island. Email to author, 9 March 2003.

NINE

THE FLORA

With the management structure in place, and finance available, the question was what to plant? There wasn't a lot to build on. Firstly, the island was so highly modified it was hard to know what had been there in the beginning, and secondly, no one had attempted such an extensive reafforestation project before.[1] In the entire Hauraki Gulf Maritime Park, only a few thousand trees were being planted each year. Craig and Mitchell wanted to replant an entire island!

No one else seemed to know much, either: when Neil Mitchell visited a local garden centre to ask about native plants, which 'hardly figured in garden centres then', he was told, 'Oh, they don't grow very well around here.'

The management team's decisions were based on the following: Tiritiri Matangi is assumed to have been covered originally in coastal broadleaf forest, containing, among others, kohekohe, taraire, pohutukawa, mapou, mahoe, whau, cabbage trees, and tree ferns.

While the Maori had cleared some land by burning, it was the farming that brought about the greatest changes: 130 years of grazing, plus regular and sometimes disastrous fires, had reduced Tiri to a 'bald island'. Vegetarian kiore had been present for centuries.

The first observations of flora and fauna were made at the building of the lighthouse. The botanist Leonard Cockayne (1855–1934) visited the island on several occasions. His 1905 notebook is cryptic: 'Tiri-Tiri Island 17 Feb 1905 … Phorm tenax on base of rocks by sea with lobelia auriceps?? Growing

The basket fungus has a remarkable structure.
Eve Manning

Left: A hillside on the Kawerau Track: flax, whau, kohekohe, mahoe, five-finger, manuka, kanuka and cabbage trees form a rich tapestry of coastal forest. Anne Rimmer

Facing page: Pohutukawa cling to the eastern cliffs.
Pat Greenfield

Pohutukawa

Early Maori would have known at least one tree that is still on Tiri today: a huge pohutukawa at the top of Bush 2. This giant once had the widest spread of any pohutukawa in New Zealand (52 metres) with a trunk circumference of 10 metres, but it collapsed during Cyclone Bola on 7 March 1988 when winds snapped off great branches. The tree is still very much alive, however, and surrounded today by the vigorous growth of young saplings. A side branch was aged to 700 years by a ring count, so the tree is about 900–1000 years old.

Hansen recorded the tree almost 100 years ago: 'Today, measured largest Pohutukawa on the Island. . . . greatest spread of branches, 118 feet [35 metres].

A well-balanced tree, and must be of enormous age. Should like to hear if you [Cheeseman] know of larger tree.'

Leonard Cockayne visited Tiri again in 1923, when he was 68, possibly to check on the effects of a recent fire. He took some photos, now in Te Papa, and he posed beside Tiri's giant. Ray Walter points out the bareness of the ground in this photograph. From the blackened trunk, plus the small ferns growing, he deduces the area had been burnt perhaps two years previously.

The Kawerau Track skirts another collapsed giant pohutukawa, which lies sprawled like an upended spider. Lower down, the track passes massive pohutukawa trunks crisscrossed with aerial roots. From Hobbs Beach one can gaze up at the complex structure of the pohutukawa roots that bind the cliff together.

Birds and bees already appreciate the nectar from the abundant red flowers of the pohutukawa, and there may soon be geckoes coming at night for the same feast.

Left: Leonard Cockayne beside Tiri's giant pohutukawa tree in 1923. Photograph by W.R.B. Oliver 28.11.1923. Museum of New Zealand, Te Papa Tongarewa, Wellington, negative number LS.008239

Jan Velvin stands beside the giant tree today. Margaret Chappell

thro' as liane. On rock, Mesemb. aust.'; 'Photo No. 8, Remnant of forest. Dysloxylum & Rapanea W.' Cockayne's comment 'this I noted on my last visit' indicates he had been to Tiri before.[2] The King sisters, who lived on Tiri from 1928 to 1936, say there were rimu trees in the pockets of bush. They also remember gathering 'mushrooms as big as plates'.

Anders Hansen collected 261 plants for the Auckland War Memorial Museum; its Cheeseman Herbarium still holds five of them. Hansen's letters to Frederick Cheeseman, the long-time curator and director of the museum, provide charming snapshots of island life:

> Whenever I am in the bush I am carefully looking for piper excelsum, but have seen none, all seem to be P. Major. It seems strange that the commonest sort should be rare or absent here, and the other common. Referring again to D. Auriculata, it appears to flower here, six–eight weeks earlier than the time given in the Flora.
>
> The work of collecting is getting very interesting to me, and I look forward to your letters with the greatest interest, always hoping something interesting may have been among the plants sent up, but even without that I like to know the names of even the commonest plants. I am very sorry I didn't begin years and years ago.
>
> I am getting more familiar with the *Manual of the New Zealand Flora* now. At first it appeared too advanced for a new beginner. . . .
>
> Will you kindly inform me if plants are packed well enough. Am sending 19 specimens. Hope there may be some rare ones among them.
>
> I remain
> Sir
> Yours very faithfully
> A. Hansen.[3]

Ferns

Tree ferns or ponga are a vital part of New Zealand forest, and a close-up view of the koru, the unfurling new shoot, reveals nature's magic. Robins and hihi (stitchbirds) gather the velvety brown hairs from the new shoots to line their nests, while moreporks and tui nest in the bowl of the tree fern, and bellbirds nest in the dead fronds on the trunk.

Although tree ferns grow well on the island, none were planted, nor were any of the smaller ferns: it would have been pointless to plant shade-loving species until the canopy was well established. Though some ferns are now returning to the darker parts of the forest, the ground still looks unnaturally bare after having been browsed out.

The pink fronds of the rasp fern (*Doodia media*) are particularly pleasing growing alongside the track. Bracken fern spread into the grasslands after Tiri was left fallow in the 1970s. Bracken shows up in early colour photos as brown patches. Takahe dig up and eat the bracken roots.

Pink fronds of the rasp fern light up the forest.
Anne Rimmer

Left: Sunlight filters through ponga fronds.
Amanda Palmer

Tropical morning glory
(*Ipomoea cairica*). Pat Greenfield

Herbarium specimen of
Ipomoea cairica (syn. *I.
palmata*) collected by Anders
Hansen, 1907. The label is
in Cheeseman's hand.

Auckland War Memorial Museum
Herbarium (AK 7383). Anne Rimmer

The morning glory, *Ipomea cairica* (which used to be called *Ipomea palmata*), is found only at Fishermans Bay. The flowers are dark purple in colour, and there is also a white version with dark blue centres. Tiritiri Matangi is the southernmost limit for this tropical plant.

Twenty-eight of Hansen's species have subsequently vanished from Tiri, with a corresponding increase in introduced plants: at the beginning of the twentieth century 22 percent of the species on Tiri were exotic but by 1981 this had increased to 45 percent.

By the 1940s, Tiri had only 6 percent forest, with 92 percent grassland, and 1 percent each of bracken and scrub. By 1973, bracken (29 percent) was encroaching on grassland (58 percent) but the amount of forest remained unchanged at 6 percent. Alan Esler, in 1970, found 166 native species of flora and recorded 343 vascular plant taxa, or groups. Carol West recalls that, in 1980, 'From a distance, the island was brown, with high bracken and grass on the ridges, and trees only in the gullies.'

Only one or two aging mature specimens of some tree species remained by the end of the farming period: there was one mangaeo (which has since died), one big totara, two puriri, one hinau, a few rewarewa. Six permanent study plots were laid down in 1972 to record changes in vegetation.

Exotic trees — wattles, pines and gums — were planted by lighthouse keepers over the years. 'The Plantation' near the lighthouse, with its huge macrocarpas and a Norfolk Island pine, was probably planted by Hansen. The trees are not present in the 1902 Winkelmann photo (page 30), but subsequently their height is useful for dating photographs. Along with the lighthouse, the 100-year-old Plantation now forms part of the silhouette of Tiri from the mainland.[4]

The wattles were probably planted as a windbreak for a keeper's vegetable garden in the 1940s. They have self-seeded throughout 'Wattle Valley' but will disappear as the native forest grows taller. The Wattle Valley area was fenced off and left to grow wild in 1975 when the lighthouse staff was downgraded to one keeper. Consequently, trees such as the grove of mahoe

Rare plants

Some rare or endangered plants are grown on Tiri. These include: kakabeak (*Clianthus puniceus*); the wood rose, pua renga (*Dactylanthus taylori*); and the Poor Knights lily (*Xeronema*). Three *Elingamita johnsonii* trees on Tiri originate on the Three Kings Islands group, as does the *Tecomanthe speciosa* vine, which luxuriates over fences in the nursery.

Tecomanthe. Pat Greenfield

Kakabeak. Val Smytheman

(whiteywood) at the start of the Wattle Track are self-seeded, and 10–20 years older than the planted forest.

Ancient pohutukawa still line the cliffs and a few big pohutukawa are dotted over the island. Where their shade had suppressed the rank grass growth, after farming ceased, clusters of young trees were growing. These had germinated from bird droppings.

Because of the fire risk from this long grass, the HGMP Board wanted urgent action. The management plan stated: 'to overcome the vigorous grass growth, rapid-growing, shade-producing species are required. … It is suggested that the reafforestation of the island be based on an "enrichment planting" with pohutukawa as the main species.'[5]

The pioneer species had to be able to withstand high winds,

Before and after: Left, 1960. Trevor Scott Below, the same view in 2004. Anne Rimmer

Below left: The bare island: an aerial photograph of Tiri in 1940. Tiri Archives

Cabbage trees

This New Zealand icon is popular with many birds: saddleback probe to the base of the leaves with their long beaks, seeking both insects and water; kakariki and other birds enjoy the nectar from the panicles of fragrant, cream flowers whose perfume fills the bush in wafts of scent in the spring; kereru eat the fruit. The trees also provide good nesting material and nest sites.

Many cabbage trees are dying from Sudden Decline Disease, which is caused by a bacterium transmitted from tree to tree by insects. The trees die swiftly, the crown withering, the bark falling off and fungus sprouting from the dying trunk, before the tree crashes to the ground. Sometimes the fallen trunk sprouts new growth. Fortunately some individuals are proving to be resistant to the disease.

Cabbage trees prefer damp conditions. The tree at the wharf shelter, for example, is standing in a stream.

Left: Dying cabbage tree on the Wattle Track. Matt Low

Cabbage-tree flowers have a sweet perfume. Anne Rimmer

drought (because there would be no watering after planting) and salt spray. Pohutukawa, a tough coastal species, could fulfil all these requirements. 'Taraire, kohekohe, mapou, matipo and manuka will be used to enhance the major plantings of pohutukawa.' The management team planned to include fruit-bearing and seed-producing trees to provide food for the birds, and flowering trees to give nectar for the honeyeaters.

The plants were to be eco-sourced, i.e. seeds were to be gathered from plants on the island, or from sources nearby, thus ensuring that the plants were best adapted to their environment. This was another progressive move that met with resistance. Some members of North Shore Forest and Bird, for example, suggested that the planting could be done much faster if people brought cuttings from their gardens.

In actual fact, the *Rhabdothamnus* seeds were obtained from Little Barrier Island and the North Island broom came from Cuvier Island. Some puriri seed was collected from the trees on Puriri Drive, Ellerslie, in Auckland. There were only two nikau palms on the island in the 1980s. Others have been introduced from Warkworth and Little Barrier. Kowhai came from Hen Island, Rangitoto Island and the Whangaparaoa Peninsula. There was some controversy over the introduction of kowhai: it was not on Tiri originally and Carol West is one who feels it should not have been planted.

Meticulous records were to be kept of every stage of this pioneering work.

The main planting period was from 1984 to 1994, during which time 280,000 trees were planted. Though initially there was an emphasis on pohutukawa, Ray Walter later realised that shrubs actually did a better job of spreading to cover the ground and from then on more shrubs, e.g. ngaio, karo, kawakawa, whau and the coprosmas, were used. Some of these short-lived plants are now coming to the end of their lifespan.

TEN

THE SPADE BRIGADE

Now came the actual growing period.

Ray Walter went to retrain as a plantsman at the Lands and Survey nursery in Taupo, finding there a valuable mentor in Herwi Scheltus. Meanwhile, the HGMP Board employed a landscape architect, Michael (Mike) Cole, who had been a lecturer at Canterbury University.

It was soon clear that Mike approached things from a different angle to that of John Craig and Neil Mitchell, and this caused some friction: 'Mike was a New Age guy with an interest in things spiritual' (he was also a trained acupuncturist), recalls Mike Lee. 'He had a very unusual approach to teaching landscape architecture,' observes Neil Mitchell. 'He brought this extra dimension of the human being in the environment, and that there's a human history to the island as well.'

'Not much is known about the propagation of many of our native species,' reported Mike Cole. 'We have tried freezing, etching, acid application and soaking.'[1] 'Ray was fantastic. He'd go out and he'd collect seeds of anything and everything. No one knew how to grow most of it, and he just tried!'[2]

It was decided that the puriri trees on Tiri were sterile and none of the seeds would grow, but Ray succeeded by putting seeds in a plastic bag or a bucket of water and forgetting about them until their outer coatings had rotted away. Then he stomped on them with his boots, after which the seeds germinated swiftly.

It was a suggestion from Herwi Scheltus that serendipitously shaped the direction of the whole project. He recommended growing the plants in 'root trainers'. These new products encouraged long fibrous roots in the young plants, but also, because they were smaller and lighter than the usual black polythene bags, anyone — even a child — could carry a tray or 'book' of them. Originally the plan had been to use experienced, specialised people to do the planting, but now the public could be involved.

But how many plants should they grow? The team used

Planters are often assisted by takahe, such as Greg.
Val Smytheman

Construction of the nursery, seen from the lighthouse in 1983.
Ray Walter

Right: On the western slopes, Mike Cole instructs an early group on planting, 1984.
Ray Walter

Walter built them with the help of three girls on a government work scheme. The young women were inexperienced builders but under Ray's supervision the nursery went up fast.

Dams in Lighthouse Valley were enlarged to provide water for the nursery. Ray would take down a can of petrol, set the pump running and leave it. When the motor quit that was the day's water supply. The project was on a tight budget: the only vehicle on the island was a 16-year-old tractor, and Ray, a trained carpenter, had been using his own tools. When he went on leave, taking his tools with him, Mike Cole had to requisition the HGMP Board for tools — even a screwdriver — to carry on.

While the nursery was being built on Tiri, the first pohutukawa seedlings were growing in Taupo from Tiri seeds. On Tiri these 1200 trees were planted out in four test plots in July 1983 by a group of Lands and Survey staff and park rangers led by Rex Mossman, the chief ranger.

Each test plot received a different treatment: one set was simply planted in a hole dug in the grass; the second set was 'released', i.e. the grass around the plant was clipped; the third group had the grass spot-sprayed with weed-killer; and the last set was both released and sprayed. All plants had a teaspoonful of fertiliser put into the planting hole, but no post-planting weed-

lateral thinking to answer this: firstly, knowing that planting could only be done in the winter months, the number of boat trips was calculated, allowing for 50 percent bad weather cancellations. A fit person can plant about eight trees per hour but in each boatload only half would be able-bodied (the frail, the elderly and children making up the other half). Thus they calculated the number of trees each boatload would be likely to plant. They estimated that 30,000 trees would be planted per year, and the nursery was built accordingly. The management team was working on the basis of a five to ten-year planting period, with a review of the process after three years.

The project received good publicity in the press, and groups were writing, offering to help with the planting, even before the seedlings were ready.

Herwi Scheltus designed the propagation house (9 by 6 metres) and shade house (20 by 9 metres), 'the whole structure capable of withstanding a 50-kilometre easterly wind' and Ray

The tractor was the only mode of transport in 1984. Elsa Laing

Far left: Mike Cole and Ray Walter in the new green-house, 1984. Ray Walter

ing or watering was done. Success was judged solely on whether the plants lived or died!

When Ray Walter went out to inspect their work next morning he was astounded to find 700 of the newly planted trees uprooted! The culprits were pukeko. John Craig decided they were just curious about something new in their territory, but Ray maintains they were checking that the trees had been planted properly. The pukeko continually inflicted a 10–20 percent tree mortality, but they also determined the final planting technique of simply digging a hole and planting the tree without any releasing. The grass hid the trees from the pukeko and also protected them from high winds.

The test plots are still being monitored at five-year intervals, but at the time nobody bothered waiting for the results. Survival was phenomenal and the project had an unstoppable momentum, with 20,000 seedlings already growing in the nursery on Tiri ready for the 1984 season.

The honour of being the first public planting group goes to Waiheke Forest and Bird, in a trip organised by Mike Lee, the founding chairman of the Hauraki Gulf branch of the Royal Forest and Bird Protection Society. Tom Frewen wrote about what was then a novel experience, in the *Gulf News*:

Putting down roots on Tiri

The 65 people who boarded the *Glen Rosa* and the *Island Princess* with their spades and packed lunches at 7.00am on Wednesday comprised the first large group to take part in a $45,000 planting scheme to restore Tiri to its natural state.

The significance of this occasion was entirely lost on the weather, which chose that day to dump the rain it had been saving for a month on Auckland and the Hauraki Gulf. Or perhaps as Tiri project manager, Mike Cole observed, raising his voice to be heard above the drumming of rain on the roof of the island's nursery, nature was looking after her own.

The 1000 pohutukawa and karaka saplings planted on Wednesday could not have had a better present than the 50 mm (1.9 in) of rain that fell on Tiri that day. The northerlies that drove the rain into the Gulf also helped to make the trip memorable.

... [The boats] lurched and rolled as they made a mountain out of every wave on the one and a half hour voyage to Tiri. ... some conservationists added another dimension to the nickname 'Greenies' ...

Ray and Barbara Walter planting in 1989. Liz Maire

A hillside of young trees, c.1986. Zane Burdett

Set aside for the Waiheke group were pohutukawa and karaka for planting on ridges and gullies near Hobbs Beach. But before they could begin, heavy rain showers forced them to retreat into the nursery …

Taking their spades, bags of 'magamp' fertiliser and wire baskets full of seedlings in long, narrow Canadian root trainers, some descended into the valleys to plant karaka while others planted pohutukawa around the tops.

The first spade into the still-dry ground beneath the soaked grass and bracken was a signal for the rain to return from its mid-morning break and planting continued for the next hour and a half in a continuous downpour.[3]

Sandra Lee-Vercoe, who almost 20 years later became Minister of Conservation, remembers that 1984 planting trip with pride but also sadness because seven-year-old Annabel, Sandra and Mike's daughter, suffered an accident on the return ferry trip, losing a finger when it was caught in a mooring rope.

There was no regular ferry service during most of the planting era and many different boats brought planters from Auckland, Devonport, and the Wade River at Whangaparaoa. Gulf Harbour Marina didn't exist in those days. Later, in the 1990s, Gulf Harbour Ferries ran a regular service until they were taken over by Fullers in 1999.

From 1967, the Hauraki Gulf Maritime Park vessels plied the Gulf. The *Ocean Star* brought all the supplies to build Tiri's nursery, and the soil to grow the 280,000 trees. Lionel Brock captained her and her successor, the purpose-built *Hauturu*. Frank Arnott, the secretary of the HGMP Board, was an ex-Navy man, 'another with salt water in his veins' as the HGMP newsletter put it. He made a valuable contribution to the designing of the *Hauturu*. Nowadays she is the DOC boat in the Gulf and calls fortnightly at Tiri, bringing supplies, passengers and provisions for the DOC staff.

In that first planting year of 1984, there were 43 boat trips and 28,900 trees were planted, increasing to 36,300 trees in 1985. On average, people planted fewer trees than expected, mainly because they were just not strong enough: Ray often found himself digging the holes for several people to plant in; but this was balanced by an increase in the number of planting trips.

Ray Walter, who still had children to care for, was joined in 1985 by a long-time family friend, Barbara Gough. 'This was the biggest surprise to us all,' remembers Neil Mitchell. 'There was this lady … very much a town-based Englishwoman … and she so fell in love with the island.' Ray and Barbara married in 1986, and have been the face of Tiri ever since.

The first planting trips had taken a work-gang approach, with people being expected to plant all day. Needless to say, many of them didn't return. Barbara Walter realised that people needed rewarding for their efforts. Groups were met at the wharf and escorted up to the nursery area to warm up. There were 'cups of tea all round with "passed-your-eyes" milk from the house cows'.[4] Mike Cole had prepared a clear, illustrated leaflet on how

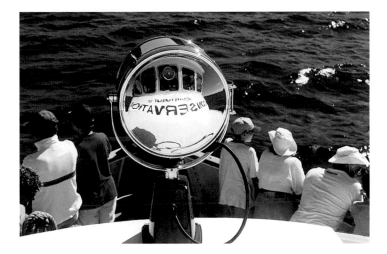

The *Hauturu*, built for the HGMP, is now the DOC boat. Zane Burdett

enal survival rate: the organisers had expected 50 percent mortality but got a 70 percent survival rate, resulting in the dense planted areas today. Professor John Ogden (associate professor of forest ecology at University of Auckland) observed drily that if the trees all grew and developed trunks one metre in diameter, 'we'll have a solid block of wood on the island'.

Each person carried a 'book' containing one tree species and walked in a straight line downhill, planting. Beside them others were planting different species. This resulted in striped hillsides which, as John Craig discovered, drew derision from critics. 'At science conferences, other scientists would show a picture. "Look at the disgusting things being done in the name of conservation in NZ. Here's Tiri, the worst example you can find."' Gordon Ell, from Forest and Bird, was one who made his planted line as irregular as he could, and later the plantings were more randomised.[6] While, aesthetically, the striping still looks odd, one doubts that the birds care, so long as they have adequate shelter and food. Ralph Silvester, a plant expert who advised Ray, feels that not enough attention was paid to varying habitats. He

to plant, which ended: 'Be assured that by your labours you are creating a treasure house for future generations.' Ray Walter demonstrated how to plant, then everyone selected their trees from the nursery and put them on the tractor's trailer. (Ray says they loved the selection part.) After following the tractor to their allotted planting site (the walk could take half an hour), they planted trees for *no more than an hour*. Older people helped in the nursery area with lighter work such as pricking out seedlings.

Elizabeth Morton, who still regularly volunteers in the shop, heard a radio announcement in 1984 — 'Take a spade and your lunch' — and went along. 'We all wore "Swannies"[5] and woolly caps. I often wondered, how would we look to boats? Armies of moving people like flowers on the hillside.' She planted 46 trees that first day, and has planted many more since.

Gael Arnold felt a great sense of spirituality to be planting on the island where her great-grandfather had been lighthouse keeper 100 years before: she is the great-granddaughter of Felix McGahey, the keeper from 1883 to 1886, and her grandfather was born during that time.

The seedlings grown onsite in the Tiri nursery were even hardier than the first batch from Taupo. This, plus the care taken in teaching people to plant properly, contributed to the phenom-

Many varieties of young trees growing in the nursery, 1992. Pat Greenfield

Scientists scoffed at Tiri's striped hillsides. John Craig

Facing page: Eric Geddes and a young helper building saddleback nesting boxes, c.1984. Anon.

would have said, 'There's a damp place here, so plant something that will grow well in damp.'

The first release of an endangered bird, the saddleback, was made in 1984. The immediate success of that transfer, with low mortality and the birds breeding within a few months of release, probably facilitated future transfers to Tiri. The saddleback remains Barbara's favourite bird.

By 1986 Ray was a full-time employee of Lands and Survey, and had become the sole guardian of the Tiri project after Mike Cole left in 1985. Despite continuing bitterness at the closure of the lighthouses, Ray was glad to be able to remain on Tiri. He had the full support of the HGMP Board and of John Craig and Neil Mitchell.

For Ray, a bittersweet incident occurred shortly after the lighthouse was automated in 1984:

> ... There was an irate telephone call in the middle of the night — one, two o'clock in the morning, and this joker said, 'Are you the lighthouse keeper on Tiri?' I said, 'No' [quietly]. He said, 'But ... this is the Tiri lighthouse telephone?' I said, 'The light is automatic. I'm no longer a lighthouse keeper!'

And he said, 'I don't care who you are! This is the Harbour Bridge Control here. Will you do something about your bloody lighthouse, because it's stopped, and it's shining light down the centre of the Auckland Harbour Bridge!' The chances of it happening — of it stopping in that right place — are about a million to one ... this bloody huge 11 million candlepower light is shining right down the centre of the bridge! He was not very happy. It had been stopped for an hour or so ... I went up the top, gave the thing a little push, and away it went again. But I thought, 'Here's your automatic light! Bugger youse!'

When Ray and Barbara Walter went off the island for a break, relievers came on to keep things running. As he left, Ray would ask, 'Now you're sure you know how to turn on the lighthouse, and milk the cow?' The relievers kept up the log:

> 8 Feb 1987: Cow, chooks, weather.
> Blowing up to 40 knots.
> 19 Feb 1987: Watered glasshouse and nursery.
> Rooster attacked Sandra in morning, me in evening.
>
> 24 Oct 1987: Pigs, chooks, goats etc.
> Radio I ringing hourly for weather reports.
> 10:30 Lady Eva arrived with 6 visitors
> 2 pm Te Aroha arrived with 15 visitors.
> Cows, chooks, goat etc.
> 1 baby chook has diahhur the shits.
> 8:30 pm Rangitoto Ranger arrived with 5 visitors.

Weather reporting has always been a part of the lighthouse keeper's job. In the 1920s the Post Office rang Tiri every day at 9 am to get an update. The meteorological instruments are housed in a white-fenced area just south of the lighthouse. In the 1980s the keepers did eight weather reports a day. Ray would call a popular breakfast show conducted by Peter Leitch, 'The Mad Butcher', on ZB radio to discuss the weather each morning. Ray still files weather reports, but no longer gets up early for a 6 am phone-in.

Thus the pattern was established: every winter for 10 years

'The Spade Brigade', as they became known, came across to Tiri and planted trees. School groups, church groups, Forest and Bird, botanical and ornithological societies, tramping clubs, scouts and guides set off early on chilly winter mornings and returned in the dark — wet and muddy — clutching their spades.

Why did they come? Neil Mitchell feels that people then had a deep desire to help with conservation, and there was nothing else competing with Tiri, whereas now there are any number of conservation projects needing help. The island had excellent PR, with the *HGMP Newsletter* keeping people informed. And people

North Island saddleback

North Island saddleback, tieke
Philesturnus carunculatus rufusater
Protected; threatened; endemic.

The Navy assisted the transfer of saddle-backs, HMNZS *Pukaki* bringing the birds from Cuvier Island in 1984. Twenty-two birds were released on Tiri on 25 February 1984 and a similar number were taken to Little Barrier. By then saddlebacks had already been successfully transferred to several offshore islands from their one remaining stronghold on Hen Island in the Hen and Chickens.

On Tiri the birds were released in five different valleys, in the forest remnants. Each group had been caught at a different location on Cuvier to preserve their song dialects and these differences remain today.

The birds used the nesting and roosting boxes that had been put up for them, and multiplied rapidly, having up to four broods a year of four chicks each (eight times the normal productivity). In 1989–90 over 100 chicks were produced. One female from the original Cuvier release was still alive and breeding in 2002 at the age of seventeen.

Saddlebacks have already been transferred from Tiri to several locations, but the population is probably reaching saturation again at around 600–700 individuals. For the translocation to Karori Sanctuary in 2002, Tim Lovegrove used a hand net to catch young birds feeding on the lighthouse lawn.

For saddlebacks to be out in the open and not in their traditional forest habitat suggests that the birds are running out of room.

The jaunty, glossy black birds with a bright chestnut saddle are often seen in family groups, busily fossicking amongst the dead leaves, or on cabbage trees, searching for insects among the leaves.

Their loud, confident calls are often the first birdsong heard on arrival, a welcome sound to regular visitors. The saddleback's softer sounds resemble those of the kokako, reminding us they are both wattlebirds. The saddleback's wattles are brilliant orange teardrops, more prominent on an adult than a juvenile. Like the kokako, they are poor flyers.

It is easy to see how vulnerable the saddle-back is to predation by mammals as it busies itself on the forest floor. It clearly has nothing in its genetic make-up to warn it there may be danger on the ground. However, being now established on 11 offshore islands, the saddle-back is no longer regarded as endangered.

North Island saddleback. Anne Rimmer

Right: *Te Aroha* at Tiri
wharf, c.1995. Zane Burdett

Below: Crowds arrive for
the Tenth Anniversary
planting day, 1994. Neil
Mitchell and John Craig,
with Ian Higgins behind
them. Zane Burdett

kept coming back because they got rewards. For Mel Galbraith the reward was to see saddlebacks, whereas Mike Lee felt that even seeing bellbirds was sufficient reward. Even then, the bird-song on Tiri was much louder and more diverse than on the mainland.

And, of course, there was the presence of Ray and Barbara Walter who, as they still do, met almost every boat, welcoming people and making each person feel special. Barbara keeps careful lists of people who have come, and is excellent at keeping in contact. Botanist Alan Esler, revisiting Tiri in 1999 after an eight-year absence, was amazed to find that Barbara not only recognised him immediately but also resumed the conversation virtually where they had left off.

Soon Tiri was so popular that the number of trees per group was rationed, and then Barbara needed a waiting list. 'So popular is Tiri … that the Hibiscus Coast Conservation and Litter Committee has been unable to arrange a tree planting expedition for this year … The Committee is now 14th on the list for next year.'[7]

Eric Walter, Ray's youngest son, attended every planting for years, and dug many holes for seniors. The lovely letters of

thanks the schoolchildren wrote to Ray and Barbara often ended with, 'Say hello to Eric'.

In 1985, the bottom keeper's house was converted into the bunkhouse. Auckland University and North Shore Forest and Bird each contributed $5000 for the modifications, which provided sleeping for 20 people and capacious kitchen and bathroom facilities. Eric Geddes and Ralph Silvester, two retired Forest and Bird members, stayed on the island quite often. Eric built many of the saddleback nesting and roosting boxes and helped with fitting out the bunkhouse, while Ralph, who had studied agriculture at the Sorbonne in Paris, helped and advised Ray in the nursery. They both recall some exciting trips over from Whangaparaoa in Eric's 'tinny' (small metal dinghy).

Graham Ussher spent a week on Tiri in 1990, after which Ray invited him back as a paid worker over his four-month university summer break. Graham's father, who worked for the Lands and Survey Department, had asked Ray to 'teach Graham how to use a hammer and drive a tractor'. Graham loved every minute of it. 'I got my hands dirty doing everything from track maintenance and wildlife work to building, plumbing, electrical, nursery and farm work. It was a fantastic introduction to practical conservation ... with the added bonus of being a stunning location and having the bunkhouse and The Bach to myself for virtually the whole summer.' For those used to the hubbub of Tiri in summer nowadays, it is hard to imagine that during the planting years the summer months were quiet.

Over the next few years Graham spent all his university breaks on Tiri working as an assistant ranger to Ray. He made 'Graham's Road', which forks off the Wharf Road. Graham, now a herpetologist, supervised the transfer of tuatara to the island in 2003.

Ruby Jones first came over on a planting weekend in 1991 and returned as a volunteer during school and university holidays. As well as nursery work, she helped Barbara with monitoring the robins and the saddlebacks — and she met Graham Ussher. From 1997 to 1999 Ruby studied the kokako for her masters degree.

A distinctive boat in the Hauraki Gulf during the 1990s was the old kauri coaster *Te Aroha*. Her owners Mike and Dee Pigneguy brought the first eco-tours to Tiri, often anchoring overnight so their passengers could enjoy both a night walk and the dawn chorus. *Te Aroha* was used for the first Supporters' picnics. The takahe, Aroha, was so named because *Te Aroha* was at Tiri on the day she hatched.

Mel and Sonya Galbraith 'had many lovely family holidays on the island' with their four young daughters. The Galbraiths would arrive *en masse* 'with high chairs, and heaps of baggage'. With fellow Glenfield College teachers Neil Davies and Graham Jones, Mel brought large groups of students over for field trips. In 1985, 102 students and two teachers set a planting record of

Dear Guardians of Tiri

Thank you for a grand day on an island which is becoming more and more exciting.

May the little trees flourish, and the birds thrive.
Yours sincerely

(Signed) R. B. Sibson.
[Letter, No Date. in Tiri archives]

'A world recreating itself with a little help from its friends.'
– WWF leaflet

Before and after:
Left: looking north from Coronary Hill, 1989.
Neil Davies
Below: 2003. Anne Rimmer

Brown teal

Brown teal, pateke
Anas aucklandica chlorotis
Protected; threatened; endemic.

Brown teals are not yet a success story on Tiri. There had been a minor release of six in 1987 and more were brought in on 8 July 1990 for a public release. 'Air-raid shelters' were made on some dams to protect the ducks from harriers. These were essentially camouflaged roofs, jutting out over the water, which the ducks could hide under — at this time the banks had little vegetation on them. The teals had been reared by Ducks Unlimited, a conservation and hunting group that focuses on improving wetlands for game birds. Although brown teals are now protected, they could be hunted up until 1921.

The teals bred well at first and within three years the population grew to about 40 birds. One night there were 16 teal carousing outside the

bunkhouse. But many ducklings were being killed by both eels and hawks, particularly after DOC ordered the removal of the air-raid shelters because they considered them untidy.

Furthermore, the young males were leaving the island because there was no suitable gathering place for them, so that each dam on Tiri had a resident and lonely female, but only one male remained on the island. The recently completed wetland area at the northern end of the island should remedy this.

When seven more teals were released by Ducks Unlimited in 2002, several were quickly killed by hawks.

Nevertheless, the breeding success in 2003 was better. Some males divided their attention between females, appearing daily at a different dam. 'Finn the Philanderer' featured in soap-opera-styled reports in the *Dawn Chorus*.

The wharf dam is the first stop on the guided walk, and visitors love seeing this shy little duck swimming across to say hello. Having been captive-reared they are tame, and remain so because Barbara Walter feeds them in order to monitor them.

Left: Ozzie, a friendly brown teal.
Barbara Hughes

Right: The Tenth Anniversary planting day, 1994. Ray Walter, Jason Boobyer, George Thew, Neil Mitchell and John Craig. Zane Burdett

1800 trees in one day. Glenfield College students later helped with the stitchbird transfer.

On 31 July 1994 the weather was magical, the ferries crossing a mirror-calm sea blanketed in thick, pale grey fog. But up on the island's slopes, now dotted with healthy young trees, the 240 planters were enjoying winter sunshine above the clouds. This was the Tenth Anniversary planting day. As a symbolic gesture the youngest and the 'most mature' planters — four-year-old Jason Boobyer, and George Thew QSM, 'age indeterminate', planted two puriri trees together. The 750 trees planted that day brought the grand total to more than 231,000 trees; but the day was mainly a celebration of the successful conclusion of an audaciously ambitious project.

By 1994 seven bird species had been introduced, the Supporters' group was well established, and Tiri was entering a new phase for, as the planting wound down, the numbers of visitors and school trips were increasing.

~

ELEVEN

SUPPORT

Many of those at the Tenth Anniversary celebrations were members of the Supporters of Tiritiri Matangi Inc., a group that had already progressed far beyond the modest aims of its founding members six years before.

The idea for a Supporters' group was hatched by Jim Battersby, a retired Presbyterian minister. He and his wife Barbie first went to Tiri with a planting group in 1988. Barbara Walter took the group to look for saddlebacks in Wattle Valley, which was then just a track of mud and cabbage tree leaves. Impressed by the hospitality and kindness of Ray and Barbara Walter, who 'inspired everyone to come and to work', the Battersbys offered to go and help for a few days.

'We were like two kids. On an island!' recalls Jim. 'We hiked through the long grass to Fishermans Bay in a howling sou'wester. We had to push against the wind. It was still a wild island — just bits were planted.'[1] They helped in the nursery, potting up seedlings into the root trainers. The black polythene in the nursery area was looking a bit tatty, but Ray said there was no money to replace it. In fact, he feared their already meagre budget would be cut further.

The government had announced the establishment of a new Department of Conservation (DOC), absorbing Lands and Survey, Wildlife, Forestry, and the Hauraki Gulf Maritime Park Board. It took some time to get going, but by April 1987, DOC was fully functional and, to the regret of many, the HGMP Board ceased to exist in 1990.

All this rearrangement affected Tiri's income. 'We were in

Jim and Barbie Battersby at the Tenth Anniversary planting day. Zane Burdett

Below: The nursery in 1985. Rex Mossman

dire straits,' recalls Ray Walter. The 'seed' money from WWF, which had given the nursery such a fine start, was exhausted. Previously, the boat fees had been treated as a 'donation', which the government matched two for one, but with the formation of DOC this major source of funding disappeared. 'Tiri is certainly the poor relation,' Ray wrote to DOC.

'I was weeding in the nursery,' recalls Jim, 'when I had this idea. All these people coming to plant! There must be some among them who'd be willing to pay some money? If a hundred people paid $20 a year that would be $2000.' He discussed it with his wife, and then with Ray and Barbara Walter. 'They seemed overjoyed! They were finding it very hard.'

Barbara supplied a list of her contacts. Thirty people attended

The Culvert Gang: Zane Burdett, Helen Holzer, Val Lincoln, Peter Lee — at Queen's Birthday Supporters' working weekend, June 1991 — so-named because they constructed culverts under the road. Zane Burdett

the first public meeting in August 1988, and 20 signed up as founding members of the Supporters of Tiritiri Matangi Inc. Jim was elected chairman, with Trevor Sampson as treasurer. Maureen Gilligan, Tim Ellison, Carl Hayson and Dell Hood were on the committee, and Chris Clark was the liaison officer with DOC. Mel Galbraith offered his services as secretary. Jim had not met Mel, but 'he was the best thing that ever happened to us,' exclaims Jim.

> The group's objectives are:
>
> a) To promote and enhance the open sanctuary at Tiritiri Matangi and to ensure the continuance of the project.
>
> b) To provide financial, material and physical support for the work at Tiritiri Matangi.
>
> c) To heighten public awareness of the existence and role of Tiritiri Matangi as an open sanctuary.
>
> d) To do all such other lawful things as are incidental or conducive to the foregoing objects or any of them.

The first Bulletin, put out by Barbie Battersby in February 1989, was a modest, two-sided A4 sheet. Membership had reached 55, with $1400 received. There was to be a Picnic Day on Sunday, 19 March, 'Another great opportunity to visit Tiritiri Matangi', and in 'News from Ray and Barbara': 'Ray has been waging war against the mynas with some success.'

Growth of the fledgling organisation was rapid: after a year, there were 150 members and $3000 in funds, and by 1991 there were 209 members and net income was over $14,000.

Ian Haines, the Supporters' honorary solicitor, recommended including a clause in the constitution allowing the group to own property. 'We'd never want to do that!' protested Jim, still thinking in terms of black polythene. The only vehicle on the island was the now 20-year-old tractor and the Supporters decided to try for a grant to buy a replacement. They applied to the Lotteries Grants Board (which required some wrestling with

'They held a meeting, putting $20 on the table, and the seeds for the Supporters of Tiritiri Matangi were sown.'

– Trevor Sampson, in *Friends of the Hauraki Gulf Maritime Park*, Issue 1, June 1990

Jim's Presbyterian conscience) and to their surprise got the grant of $9000, but on condition that the vehicle was owned by the Supporters, not by DOC. 'There was great excitement when the four-wheel-drive farm bike and trailer arrived . . . It made a big difference. Ray could get around much faster.'[2] The Supporters bought other practical things like timber for the Wattle Track, and a head for the sprayer; Ray was now waging war on honeysuckle.

Members of the Supporters took every opportunity to go planting on Tiri. On one trip about 120 people set a new record by planting 2000 trees in two-and-a-half hours.

The whitehead release in 1989 was the first public release of a rare bird in New Zealand. Organised by the Supporters, it was attended by over 280 people, including 60 Supporters. The birds arrived by helicopter, and groups of people accompanied the cages to five separate release sites.

No one from DOC's Auckland office attended this release, though John Craig subsequently persuaded Richard Sadlier from DOC in Wellington to come. Similarly, no one from DOC (apart from Ray Walter) had attended the previous release of brown teals.

The saddlebacks released in 1984 were doing so well that

Eric Geddes had to make 60 more nesting boxes at a cost of $400. By 1990 there were even enough birds to give some away: six saddlebacks were sent to Mount Bruce and six more to Otorohanga Native Bird Park. Forty saddlebacks that went to Karori Sanctuary in 2002 are now happily populating Wellington's suburbs.

As the Supporters grew in numbers, the bunkhouse was in greater demand for visitor accommodation, and the Supporters funded practical things like fridges, freezers, dryers and even mattresses.

Visitor numbers were up (8500 in 1991) and school trips were increasing. Glenfield College continued its 15-year association, with the entire sixth and seventh forms coming on 'The Tiri Trip' each year. Kristin School pupils raised $310 in 1990 through a mufti day and cake stalls. They bought 20 litres of paint, and 13 second-form girls spent three days painting the bunkhouse roof. Kristin School also made the track from Hobbs

Beach up to Bush 1 and later funded a huge water tank. In recognition of the school's contributions, Barbara Walter named a takahe Kristin.

The takahe release in 1991 was achieved only after years of lobbying. John Craig and Neil Mitchell had been pushing for takahe since the inception of the open sanctuary, but the authorities refused to take the request seriously. John even went down to see the Minister of Conservation in Wellington. A bird transfer does not come cheap. However, Greg Chalmers, the agricultural products technical marketing representative for DuPont (New Zealand) Ltd, had become involved with Tiri over weed control. He had already donated a $US5000 ($NZ9000) prize to Tiri and now, with his advocacy, DuPont funded the takahe release. The donation of $16,513.76 ($US9000) was given directly to the Tiri Supporters, a move that did not please DOC. One takahe of the second transfer in 1994 was renamed Greg in honour of Greg Chalmers.[3]

Kristin School pupils painted the bunkhouse roof in 1990.
Friends of the Hauraki Gulf Maritime Park, December 1990

Whitehead

Whitehead, popokatea
Mouhoua albicilla
Locally common; endemic.

Eighty birds were introduced from Little Barrier Island (40 on 3 September 1989 and 40 on 29 May 1990). Dave Allen, studying the whiteheads for a thesis, had to demonstrate that he could keep the birds alive in an aviary before the transfer was authorised.

These bright-eyed little birds travel through the forest in groups, their busy buzzing indicating that a flock is nearby. Their rich, rolling song gives them their alternative name of bush canary. The male's pure white

head looks as though it has been dunked in white paint, and contrasts well with the bright black eyes and trim little beak. Females and juveniles are more subdued in plumage.

On Tiri whiteheads breed in their first adult year — a year ahead of the normal pattern. They are the main North Island host species for the long-tailed cuckoo (see cuckoo box, page 62) but, since they have their first clutch in August before the cuckoo returns, it is only the second brood that is parasitised.

Whiteheads are now the most abundant bird species on the island, numbering several hundreds. In 2003 the ARC team, led by Tim Lovegrove, captured 40 whiteheads on Tiri

for release in the Hunua Ranges (released 12 April 2003) where all bird species benefit from the predator control done for the kokako population.

Male whitehead. Peter Craw

The release drew an enthusiastic response from the public. On special days such as this the normal limit of 150 visitors is lifted, and on 26 May 1991, a crowd of 600 gathered to welcome the two birds. Mel Galbraith describes how an expectant hush came over the crowd when the helicopter was heard. Following brief speeches the two takahe, Stormy and Mr Blue, were carried around and shown to the people before being released into their temporary holding pens. Dick Veitch comments that a public release of 'big blue birds' into pens has an advantage over, say, the whitehead release where the little birds hurtled out of the box and into the trees.

Tiri's new arrivals were front-page news for weeks, especially after Mr Blue proved to be such a personality: 'Mr Blue is particularly people-oriented and likes following visitors around.' This was most unexpected as he had been described as 'rather solitary' on Maud Island. 'Used to being on his own, he is likely to be rather retiring and shy to begin with.'[4] How wrong they were!

The newspapers had poured scorn on the absurdity of DOC's supplying two male birds to start a takahe breeding programme, so when Stormy and Mr Blue built a nest and subsequently hatched a fostered egg, the paparazzi went wild.[5] Headlines: 'Takahe Foster Hopes for Breeding', 'Romance in the Air', and 'Dads Rule the Takahe Roost' accompanied front-page photos of Mr Blue feeding little Matangi. (See Chapter 16, 'Takahe — Ambassadors for the Endangered'.)

Another takahe is named Bellamy. The British scientist and TV personality David Bellamy was the guest speaker at the Supporters' Tenth Anniversary dinner in 1998. He had first visited 10 years earlier when filming 'Moa's Ark'. Sir David Attenborough has also been twice to Tiri, filming some of *The Life of Birds* there in 1996. Guest speakers at Supporters' AGMs have included Don Merton, famed for his work in saving endangered species in New Zealand, and the respected wildlife photographer, Geoff Moon, who illustrated *The Singing Island* (a book on Tiri) in 1998; his wife Lynette wrote the text.

When Jim Battersby resigned as chairman of the Supporters in 1992, Trevor Sampson took over, followed by Dell Hood.

By 1992 it was 10 years since WWF had become involved in the Tiri project, and the Duke of Edinburgh, as President of WWF, flew in to check on progress. Ray and Barbara Walter greeted the Duke and his entourage. Prince Philip was highly intrigued by the tale of the paired male takahe.

As Tiri's forest became established, more bird releases were possible. Doug Armstrong oversaw the 1992 translocation of the North Island robins, which was funded by the Supporters with a grant from the New Zealand Lottery Grants Board.

The Supporters were runners-up in the 1992 Ecotourism awards, showing how swiftly the Tiri project had become established. Tiri was a busy island: $11,000 was obtained from ENZA (an apple marketing board) in 1993. Further grants in 1994 bought another four-wheel-drive vehicle and, in 1996, a ute.

The arrival of little spotted kiwi in 1993 was an event equal in excitement to the takahe release. Again hundreds of people gathered, and, for the first time, Maori were involved in the release ceremonies: local iwi accompanied the birds from Kapiti

Greg Chalmers and John Craig at the takahe release, 1991. A. Davies

Above left: David Bellamy with Ray and Barbara, 1998. Mel Galbraith

Facing page: Mr Blue steals his lunch, c.1995. Anon., courtesy Mike and Dee Pigneguy

Dick Veitch, DOC, with children at the Kiwi release, 1993. Neil Davies

Far right: Members of the Disabled Sailing Trust at 'the Bandstand' in 1993. It took several hours to get the group to this spot. Barbara Walter

Shaun Dunning on the wharf in 2000. Anne Rimmer

Island, and they were welcomed to Tiri by local kaumatua. The Minister of Conservation, Denis Marshall, travelled with the kiwi. Mel Galbraith counts it as a highlight of his long involvement with Tiri that he personally released one of the birds into its burrow.

The kiore eradication in September 1993 (after the kiwi were released) was 100 percent successful, and the island's flora and fauna showed immediate improvements. (See Chapter 12, 'The Unwanted'.)

Shaun Dunning first went to Tiri reluctantly in 1994 with the Whitianga Conservation Corps.[6] The 16-year-old did not relish the prospect of spending two weeks on an island, and actually contrived to miss the boat over to Tiri. However, it was so enjoyable once he arrived that he asked Ray if there was ongoing work. 'There was a month doing weeds. Then the money stopped and I just never left.' Shaun lived on Tiri for almost six years. He picked up 'a bit of money from DOC and a bit from the Supporters', and then had monthly contracts with DOC. He was a full DOC employee for only the last year. How did he survive? Shaun says he lived for free in the bunkhouse, and he ate the leftovers in the fridge. This isn't as grim as it sounds because weekend visitors often leave extra food rather than carrying it off

with them; and when the motherly types among the Supporters cottoned on, they prepared extra food for the likeable and hardworking teenager. Shaun learned later that his mother and Ray Walter had had many phone conversations about his welfare.

Shaun says he was happy to be 'the dogsbody', doing 'a bit of mechanics, mowing the lawns — I like mowing lawns' — a good thing because they took five days every month. He actually got the DOC uniform before he became a DOC employee, after having had trouble exerting his authority over a difficult boatie.

Self-taught in computers, Shaun dragged Tiri into the electronic age, though the single phone line was a problem. Barbara wouldn't let him have a TV in the bunkhouse, so he fitted a card into his computer to watch TV in secret. Ray wasn't impressed when the generator was still running at 4 am so Shaun and the researchers could play computer games. Nethertheless, everyone was sorry to see Shaun leave Tiri in 2000. He still works for DOC and returns to Tiri frequently.

Ray has a knack of being able to find a job for anyone who offers, and of making them feel their contribution has been valuable. And nothing is too much trouble for him. Members of the Disabled Sailing Trust came over three or four years in a row. In 1993, Ray asked the nine young people and 14 helpers to help build a bridge at the start of the Kawerau Track. He describes the youngsters, out of their wheelchairs in the bush, cheerfully using whatever means they could to propel themselves along the ground so they could haul the timbers into place.

Just getting the group onto the island had been a mission. They arrived on the *Rotoiti* well after dark. It was blowing 25 knots and Ray didn't think they'd be able to land. This news was greeted with roars of protest from the kids, so Ray set to, 'chairs and all'. As the boat pitched up and down on the swells, they'd grab a wheelchair off the back and run up the wharf with it. 'It was pitch black.' Ray tied the chairs, with their occupants in them, onto the tractor — three chairs across the carrier box and six on the trailer. 'And they loved it!'

Ray took them down to Hobbs Beach 'to make sandcastles'. One by one, the kids sat in the cab of the tractor and learnt how to drive the front-end loader. 'The beach looked like it had been ploughed.'

In 1994, Tiri's familiar blue Ford tractor, parked outside Ray and Barbara's house, exploded, shooting flames nine metres into the air. Even after the blaze was under control the diesel fuel could be heard still boiling in the tank. Tiri was left without transport for a few weeks, during which everything had to be pushed up the hill on wheelbarrows — an exhausting task.

On 6 February 1994, a crowd of about 120 gathered for the official opening of the Kawerau Track. Graeme Campbell, DOC's Auckland regional conservator, cut the ribbon. He described the boardwalk as epitomising the role of conservation in *protecting* our natural heritage as well as making it accessible. No other volunteer project in New Zealand, he said, had ever built anything comparable.

The track and boardwalk, through mature stands of forest, had taken four years to build. Ray praised the 13-year-olds from Kristin School who had 'laboured' to carry the first load of timber from the barge up the hill to the boardwalk's beginning, and Mark Holland, who hammered 'the first nail, and the last, and a few in between'. Mark's group had come out for weekends,

Little spotted kiwi

Little spotted kiwi
Apteryx owenii
Endangered; endemic.

Little spotted kiwi were released on 4 July 1993, 'Kiwi Independence Day'. Five pairs of birds were brought from Kapiti Island, the last stronghold of this smallest of kiwis. After they were shown to the crowd, the kiwi were released into prepared burrows at various sites. Each bird was fitted with a transmitter, and PhD student Sibilla Girardet tracked their movements at night. The males roamed widely, one travelling from the north of the island to the lighthouse and back in one night (about 4 kilometres).

Three more pairs of kiwi arrived from Kapiti Island on 9 July 1995. A 1997 census by DOC scientists Hugh Robertson and Rogan Colbourne, using trained dogs, estimated the population to be 25 birds. The biggest female weighed 1.9 kilograms. The 2002 census estimated there were about 50 kiwi on the island, including three from the original release. The heaviest female ever recorded, at 2.04 kilograms, prompted the suggestion that the Tiri birds should be renamed the 'medium spotted kiwi'.

It is now very common to hear kiwi at night, even around the bunkhouse, and many sightings are made. Kiwi probe holes can be seen on some tracks and on Hobbs Beach.

Above: Ray and Barbara Walter with Tiri's 'medium spotted kiwi'. Rogan Colbourne

Little spotted kiwi. Simon Fordham

North Island robin

North Island robin, toutouwai
Petroica australis longipes
Protected; endemic.

Tiri's robins came from an exotic pine plantation on the Mamaku Plateau near Rotorua. Forty-four birds were released on 12 April 1992, and a further 14 females were brought a year later (12 April 1993). Five of these originals survived at least 10 years. Doug Armstrong and John Ewen showed that Tiri's robins were living only in about 15 hectares of the older forest on Tiri. When these areas became 'full' some juvenile birds died each winter.

Consequently, 21 birds were moved to Wenderholm Regional Park in March 1999; and a further 30 went to Great Barrier Island in April 2004. As the planted bush areas on Tiri mature, the robin population should increase.

The inquisitive robin is usually encountered on the boardwalks (researchers feed them mealworms to tame them). If an area is cleared of leaf litter, exposing the invertebrates, the birds will fly down and start feeding unconcernedly. In close-up one can marvel at the long, thin legs. Robins tremble one leg as they feed, in order to sense and entice the invertebrates below the surface. A white patch of feathers just above the bill

flashes when a bird is stressed or agitated.

Robins are territorial and occasionally neighbouring birds will squabble. The song is a descending scale of loud, ringing notes with a short twitter at the end.

North Island robin. Val Smytheman

When the tractor blew up in 1994 the only transport on Tiri was wheelbarrows. Ray Walter

completing the Wattle Track boardwalks by 1989, and then building the longer Kawerau Track. Known as 'The Coruba Club', they partied as hard as they worked. The boardwalk's pleasant, meandering quality is due to there having been no plans. Each morning the volunteers asked Ray where they should build that day. 'Oh, just put a few steps up there,' Ray would reply, with a vague wave of his hand. They went the wrong way once, but the detour was cheerfully incorporated into the design.

Though Barbie Battersby died in 1997, Jim Battersby continues his association with the island as a guide. He sees the hand of God in the success of the Supporters, saying he could not have devised it without divine help. 'It is given to few to see an idea conceived, and brought to birth, to go through childhood and into maturity: that is Tiri's gift to me.'

TWELVE

THE UNWANTED

'The island is predator-free, that is of unnatural predators. … Please be rodent-aware … we know of three instances where mice have been introduced to islands in bags. … And you children, if you have mice in your sandwiches, please take them home with you.' – Ray Walter's talk to visitors

Tiri is extremely fortunate to have had only one mammalian predator, the kiore, in its history — but only continual vigilance can keep it predator-free. The major threat to New Zealand birdlife comes from rodents (rats and mice), and mustelids (ferrets, weasels and stoats).

To understand why mammalian predators have such a devastating effect on New Zealand's birds, we must go back in time: New Zealand separated from Gondwanaland after birds evolved, but before marsupials or mammals appeared. Thus, as the New Zealand birds further evolved on their drifting ark, they had no four-legged predators to contend with; death might come from the sky — in the form of a hawk, an owl, or a giant eagle — but no cat, dog, rat or stoat pounced on birds on the ground, and no rat or stoat sidled into nests to eat the eggs and chicks or attack the parent birds.

This explains the extraordinary tameness of so many New Zealand birds. They have no reason to fear us, no ancestral memory that sounds a warning to them. Thus the saddleback, although able to fly, is perfectly happy foraging on the ground where it feels totally safe. It also nests on or near ground level, as do the kakariki and fernbird. Other New Zealand birds evolved to become flightless: the kiwi, weka, takahe, moa and kakapo — again, because flight was not necessary in the comparative safety

of prehistoric New Zealand — and these birds spend their whole life at ground level.

Then one mammal — humans – arrived, unwittingly bringing destruction with them. Maori brought the kiore (*Rattus exulans*) and dogs. Then, with Europeans came, in succession: the large Norway rat *(Rattus norvegicus)*, the mouse (*Mus musculus*), the sleek ship rat (*Rattus rattus*), which can climb trees; and then, the mustelids: the ferret (*Mustela furo*), the weasel (*Mustela nivalis vulgari*) and the stoat (*Mustela ermina*). Stoats, introduced as rabbit control in 1882, are the scourge of New Zealand's native birds. They are vicious, so cunning that they are extremely

Despite their small size (34 – 40 centimetres long including the tail), stoats are vicious predators. DOC

'*These islands are lifeboats where species have taken refuge. But when a boat sinks and people get into the lifeboats, you don't say, "Well, they're all right now." They really have to go home. To be successful it has to achieve the end of repopulating the mainland.*'

– Jim Holdaway

difficult to trap or poison, and since they can climb trees they are able to predate nests. Fortunately the Tiri channel is too wide and too rough for stoats to swim across.

In the course of a few hundred years, humans had changed the rules for New Zealand's native populations, at a pace that evolution, a slow process, could not hope to adjust to.[1] New Zealand's birds were helpless against the onslaught and fell before it in appalling numbers. In what Dr Stella Frances called 'the quiet holocaust', 42 of New Zealand's 96 species of birds have been driven to extinction since the arrival of humans over 800 years ago. Several others teeter on the brink today: the South Island kokako, orange-crowned parakeet, yellowhead, rock wren, and some species of kiwi.

From 1894, Richard Henry made a noble attempt to save New Zealand's endangered birds, finding and capturing hundreds of kakapo and kiwi and transferring them to Resolution Island in Dusky Sound, Fiordland. Henry, a bushman, had been given the job of curator and caretaker of the island after the government set it aside as a reserve. But his efforts were all for naught: when stoats reached Fiordland in 1900 (just 18 years after they had been introduced to New Zealand), they easily swam to the island, and subsequently all the flightless birds there were killed.

Tiri visitors sometimes suggest that New Zealand birds are 'stupid' in being unable to adapt to predators, but this is not so. Our birds evolved over thousands of years in a predator-free environment. Humans changed the rules in an evolutionary instant, and we must now make amends as best we can.

Predator-free offshore islands such as Tiritiri, Cuvier, Stephens and Maud Islands have become 'life rafts' for our most endangered native species: the North and South Island saddlebacks, the takahe, the stitchbird, the little spotted kiwi, and most famously of all, the black robin.[2] Don Merton, the DOC scientist whom Derek Grzelewski described as having been 'an ambulance man for endangered birds ... for the past forty years', was the leader in many of these exceptional rescues.

'Mainland islands' extend this concept. Here a suitable piece of land, often a peninsula (as at Tawharanui Regional Park and Russell Peninsula) or land otherwise isolated, for example by rivers (as at Wenderholm Regional Park), is first surrounded by traps and possibly a predator-proof fence, after which all the predators inside the area are removed. From then on, provided the defences are not breached, the area is a virtual island that, when the habitat has been sufficiently restored, can be repopulated with native birds. Karori Sanctuary in Wellington and Trounson Kauri Park near Dargaville are other mainland islands.[3] The concept is effective but extremely expensive, and should be regarded only as a temporary measure, not the long-term solution.

But it takes only one mistake for a disaster to occur: in Waitangi Park (not a mainland island, but a rich kiwi habitat), one stray alsatian in 1987 killed over 500 of the 900 brown kiwi living there in a six-week rampage. The dog averaged 12 kiwi a day until it was finally shot.

Despite several shipwrecks and considering the number of boats that have called at Tiri for 140 years, it is interesting that only one incident of ship or Norway rats has ever been recorded on Tiri. The exception is a 1962 unpublished report to the Wildlife Service by a relieving keeper, Alan Wright: 'Three rats (*Rattus*) were caught by the keepers around the houses and poison is still being laid by them.' While kiore are also '*Rattus*' *exulans*, Wright (who later joined the Wildlife Service) continues: 'One kiore was seen in the grass ...' which implies that the rats caught by the keepers were other than kiore. Just in case it happens again, traps are maintained around Tiri's coastline. These 'yellow submarines' can be seen on the wharf, and tucked in the bush.

Up to 1971, Tiri carried sheep, cattle and some pigs, and a herd of at least 40 goats ran wild at the northern end. These animals degraded the environment both by browsing and through soil compaction as they moved around. Rabbits, anathema to any farmer, were once abundant, but vanished in the early 1900s. (See Chapter 3, 'The Pastoral Century'.) There were also feral cats at that time. Anders Hansen observed: 'Wild cats are on the increase, and I hardly know how to deal with them.' Lighthouse keepers kept cats until the 1960s, when they were prohibited.

KIORE

Kiore were on Tiri for hundreds of years and, while they undoubtedly affected the original flora and fauna, a balance was achieved over time. When Tiri was left fallow after 1971, kiore numbers exploded to some of the highest rodent densities ever recorded: about 120 per hectare in the bush, rising to 200 per hectare in the grass. But when their food ran out in winter the plague of starving rodents stripped much vegetation down to bare stems, gnawing all the bark off shrubs and snapping off seedlings at ground level. 'In the winter they would come out on the lawn by the tower and eat the grass ... in the middle of the day. They had no hair on their backsides and [were] full of fleas.'[4] Kiore strolled through the bunkhouse, and ran across the faces of sleeping people in the university hut. They were so famished that the students studying them had to check their traps during the night or their study subjects had died by morning.

But when it was realised that the kiore was having major

A novelty

During the planting period, 'the little rats were a hit with tree planters for whom they were a novelty. . . . Discovery of a kiore in the thick grass would inevitably set off squeals of excitement amongst the volunteers.'[5] And Ray Walter entertained schoolchildren by releasing a rat into a circle of kids.

effects on Tiri's environment, and advances in technology made an eradication feasible, it was decided that this 'rather attractive and vegetarian native rat' (as one newspaper unthinkingly described it) had to go. Extensive studies were done beforehand on how each bird species would respond to the poison bait and the three takahe, plus two pairs of brown teal, were rounded up. The recently introduced kiwi were presumed to be at no risk from the bait, and this proved to be correct. Over two tons of brodifacoum, an anticoagulant, was dropped from a helicopter by Tony Monk of Helitranz on 29 September 1993. This single poison drop produced a 100 percent kill rate. Seven native bird species suffered some mortality, the pukeko population plummeting to only 12 birds, which halted several scientific studies on them.

Starving kiore gnawed the bark off every sapling, c.1980. John Craig

Above left: Kiore on Cuvier Island, 1986. Dick Veitch

Left: A kiore runs up a ponga trunk. John Craig

The positive effects were immediate: North Island broom, kohekohe and other plant species showed a marked improvement, skink and insect numbers increased and kakariki and quail enjoyed population booms.

This success on Tiri facilitated eradication of kiore and rats on the much larger island of Kapiti with two poison drops in 1996. We may think of our island sanctuaries as pristine, but Little Barrier Island had feral cats until 1981 and was infested with kiore until this year. A poison drop was done there in June 2004, but its success will not be known for two years.

ARGENTINE ANTS

In 2000 DOC entomologist, Chris Green, noticed a column of unusual ants on a tree near the wharf. He identified Argentine ants (*Linepithema humile*), 'one of the world's most invasive and problematic ant species'. They are presumed to have come to Tiri during the construction of the new wharf in 1998. Though small, sheer weight of numbers enables the Argentine ant to take over from native ant species.

The ants were found only around the wharf area except for one smaller population at Northeast Bay. This happened because Shaun Dunning had taken the dinghy over on the truck to do some work near Northeast Bay. Unfortunately, in the dinghy was a big nest of ants. It is a good thing that the stowaways hung on tight, because eradicating ants all across the island would have been much harder.

The eradication process involved hand-laying baits at two- to three-metre intervals on a grid pattern. It took many experts, a team of helpers and the right weather, but the exercise was successful in wiping out most of the ants. By 2004, Chris Green reported finding only two small nests, whereas 'previously there were so many ants living under the wharf shed that it was a bonus to see it still there each time I visited — I half expected to see it moved off its foundations and heading off down the beach.'

Fire

With Tiri being such a dry island, there is a fire risk. Smoking is forbidden except at the wharf and in the nursery area, and barbecues and fires are prohibited. During the farming period some burn-offs got away, destroying much of the native bush and undoubtedly killing many birds and invertebrates. Fire risk increased after farming ceased and the grass grew. The HGMP got the lighthouse keeper to mow a wide firebreak along the ridge of the island. Another firebreak is in the Wattle Valley (it is a convenient shortcut to the road). Dams were built in the 1980s both for firefighting and to help the brown teal by giving them separate wetland areas: breeding pairs need their own space.

Fire! When the old 'chookhouse' was burned in 1955, lighthouse keepers had to warn the authorities that the fire was deliberate. Trevor Scott

WEEDS

Weeding has become very important in conservation practice. Shaun Dunning made it a priority while he was on Tiri, and the current DOC officer, Ian Price, is passionate about 'the unfashionable, "nasty" side of conservation'. Weeds compete strongly with the low forest on the island, and Ian believes that if we walked away from Tiri, in 10–15 years weeds would be well on the way to destroying all our work. The art of weeding is physically demanding, monotonous and requires dedication. Many thousands of weeds are removed or sprayed yearly.

Japanese honeysuckle is one of the worst weeds. By the 1980s the Wattle Valley area was being smothered under honeysuckle, an escapee from the keepers' gardens. Several herbicides were tried without success, until DuPont supplied a new product, Escort. This did the trick, even where plants had climbed so high that Ray had to spray upwards. Even so, 1937 infestations were found when the island was grid-searched in 1998. (This involves teams walking methodically through an area, searching and destroying weeds as they go.)

Substantial grants from the New Zealand Lottery Grants Board (for example, $15,000 in 2001) have funded much of the weed work. Boxthorn occurs on Tiri's cliffs, and on Little Wooded Island. Seabirds sometimes get impaled on the thorns and die. The weeders have to abseil down to reach the boxthorn plants growing on the cliffs. Many of these are so large that they have to be cut with a chainsaw.

Blue tags mark the locations of weeds found on Tiri and 230 sites have been put onto GPS (Global Positioning System), which enables weeders to find each site, even in dense bush, when they return in subsequent years to pull up the seedlings. The GPS is accurate to within five metres.

The Weed Team of 2004: Peter Craw, Vivienne Milton, Helen Lindsay and Melinda Habgood (absent Laura Young).

Ian Price

Island care

Gael Arnold started Island Care after tree planting on Tiri in 1989. She was upset at the mess ('plastic, rubbish') she saw on the shore, and determined to do something about it. Now, each year, Island Care volunteers spend a day cleaning up 47 islands in the Hauraki Gulf.

THIRTEEN

THE NON-BIRDS

Only in New Zealand would it be possible to group all non-avian fauna — the non-birds — into a single chapter.

Most people come to Tiri to look at the birds with, perhaps, a passing glance at the trees. But without the substructure of the invertebrates few birds would survive: whitehead forage among the leaves for insects; fantails catch moths on the wing; tui chase cicadas; swallows hawk over dams and grasslands; and robins grub for worms in the moist leaf litter.

Insect damage on leaves is obvious on Tiri. (No insecticides are used because insects provide food for birds.) The kawakawa looper caterpillar creates lace on every kawakawa leaf, the hole and notch caterpillar writes the 'Morse code' dot-dash pattern on flax leaves, while the chafer beetle relishes the succulent new leaves of karaka and also chomps on five-finger.

Muehlenbeckia

The common copper butterfly is one of many creatures that frequent the pohuehue, small-leaved Muehlenbeckia, (*Muehlenbeckia complexa*). The caterpillar feeds on its leaves and flowers but birds also make use of the plant: kakariki nest in the dense clumps, and pukeko use the mounds as viewpoints. Pohuehue is a determined climber in sunlit areas, and has smothered many small trees and shrubs.

Common copper butterfly. Chris Green

Cicadas, the sound of a New Zealand summer, intrigue overseas visitors. The chorus cicada, kihiwawa (*Amphipsalta zealandica*), is prevalent on Tiri. The larval stage, or nymph cicada, spends many years underground eating sap from the roots of trees, before metamorphosing into the adult cicada. The translucent cast skin is left attached to the tree trunk.

Only a few butterflies are present on Tiri: small copper and blue butterflies flit amongst the grass. The large orange and black monarch butterflies (*Danaus plexippus plexippus*) were probably self-introduced to New Zealand in 1873. Their caterpillars are equally striking, their stripes warning birds that they are unpalatable. They consume vast quantities of an introduced milkweed plant, which is grown in the nursery area.

It was not known what the endemic red admiral butterfly (*Bassaris gonerilla*) and the yellow admiral (*Bassaris itea*) ate on

Left: A chorus cicada on a cabbage tree.
Chris Green

Facing page: Visitors had close-up views of the tuatara at the release on Labour Day, 2003.
Amanda Palmer

A tree weta's spiky armour is for defence. Chris Green

Above right: Peter Taylor reported seeing green geckos on Tiri in the 1960s (photo not taken on Tiri). Tony and Jenny Enderby

Right: A moko skink, one of two species on Tiri. Matt Low

Tiri. Then, in 1991, Graeme Hambly found their host plant, a nettle (*Parietaria debilis*), growing at Pohutukawa Cove.

Weta are much-maligned insects. Though fierce-looking, their strong armour and spiky legs are mainly for defence. Nevertheless, visitors usually shudder when they see one asleep in the little weta houses. Weta are the mice of the New Zealand bush, coming out at night to clean up the debris on the forest floor. As with many insect species, their numbers rebounded after the kiore eradication in 1993. There are three species on Tiri: the Auckland tree weta (*Hemideina thoracica*); the ground weta (*Hemiandrus furcifer*); and a species of small cave weta. Chris Green would like to introduce the giant weta, wetapunga (*Deinacrida heteracantha*), which can weigh up to 70 grams — 'bigger than a song thrush'.[1] The wetapunga's last stronghold is on Little Barrier Island.[2]

Honeybees took over a big kaka nesting box soon after it was put up in Bush 1. Shaun Dunning took over 14 kilograms from the hive over three seasons, before climbing up (in beekeeping gear) to destroy the hive. Spectators scattered swiftly when it dropped and shattered, sending bees everywhere.

In 2001 a large swarm of bees on the Tiri wharf prevented the ferry docking until Ray could clear the bees away. Since he is allergic to bees, this was a risky exercise. Meanwhile, the ferry, full of schoolchildren, slowly circumnavigated the island, giving everyone a fascinating look at the far side. When the passengers finally disembarked, they still had to walk through a cloud of bees that were determined to stay on the wharf.

The native banded kokopu fish (*Galaxias fasciatus*) inhabits several streams, most notably the Kokopu Pool on the Kawerau Track. A 2001 survey found 14 banded kokopu, along with seven eels. Since eels eat the brown teal ducklings, their numbers have been controlled by trapping.

There may never have been any amphibians on Tiri and there are no plans to introduce any because of the dry climate.

Reptiles are also scarce. There are only two species of skink: the copper skink (*Cyclodina aenea*) and the moko skink (*Oligosoma moco*) and possibly a few individuals of one gecko species. Skinks can live in many different habitats, in high numbers. Copper skinks reach densities of about 15,000 per hectare in grassland and about 10,000 per hectare in planted areas. Skinks can be seen running across the path or sunning themselves, and young ones tumble like puppies in the dry leaf litter. The large populations of skinks on Tiri support many kingfishers, and now the tuatara as well.

DOC has been doing successful lizard transfers for 15 years (a shorter time than bird transfers). Graham Ussher is keen to return more lizard species to the island, especially some of the larger ones. Originally there were probably 12 species of lizards and one tuatara on Tiri. The return of the tuatara in 2003 was a significant event.

Lizards eat insects and may be important plant pollinators. If geckoes were introduced to Tiri, the flowers of nectar-bearing trees such as pohutukawa would be pollinated at night by geckoes coming to sip the nectar. Elsewhere, gecko densities of up to 150 per cubic metre have been recorded on flowers. Lizards also play a part in seed dispersal by eating fruit and excreting the seeds.

Bats, the only New Zealand mammal, were supposedly present on Tiri in small numbers at least until the 1960s, although none of the early Tiri residents interviewed had seen one. Bats purportedly roosted in the wartime FOP tower, which was blown up in 1966. There have been a few sightings since then: John Craig and Graham Jones saw a bat in a cave at Fishermans Bay in 1976, while Eric Walter and Graham Ussher saw one with a 30-centimetre wingspan flying under the wharf at dusk in January 1993.

The Supporters are funding research with a view to reintroducing bats, probably the endangered short-tailed bat (*Mystacina*

Tuatara

Northern tuatara
Sphenodon punctatus
Endemic; endangered.

Tuatara were reintroduced to Tiri on 25 October 2003 in a public release. Sixty individuals (34 females and 26 males) were transported in mailing tubes from Middle Island in the Mercury Islands group. Three of the females were carrying eggs. The reptiles were fitted with electronic marking tags for identification.

The tuatara were released in several locations, including the Kawerau Track, with half of them being put into prepared burrows. The tuatara like to bask motionless in a patch of sunlight. They will catch and eat most things that pass their way — including a saddleback! There have been many sightings since the release, both in daytime and at night. Four tuatara have been seen at once, while another person saw a kiwi and a tuatara almost simultaneously.

Tuatara means 'peaks on their backs'.

The long-lived tuatara is a unique creature; not a lizard, but the sole living member of a major group of reptiles largely unchanged since the dinosaur era, 225 million years ago.

Tuatara are in the archaeological record of Tiri, and prior to 2003 were possibly last seen on the island by a lighthouse keeper c.1902.

Sales of this magnificent life-size bronze tuatara raised funds for Tiri's replanting 20 years ago.
Anne Rimmer

tuberculatus). Few attempted bat transfers have been successful, mainly because bats have such a good homing instinct. Short-tailed bats have a close relationship with a rare plant, the wood rose (*Dactylanthus*), which has been planted on Tiri. The bat pollinates the plant when it comes to drink the sweet nectar.

Above left: Research is being done with a view to releasing short-tailed bats (photo taken under infrared light). Stefan Greif

~

FOURTEEN

THE PARALLEL UNIVERSE

One of the first things visitors notice on Tiri is the coloured tags on trees: Ray tells them the pink ones are girl trees, but really these tags are the outward sign of a hidden part of Tiri, the parallel universe of the researcher. While visitors must perforce stay on the path, the tags mark secondary tracks that loop up and down valleys and into the depths of the bush. On them may be nesting boxes, an insect trap, seed traps, artificial nests for a predation study, or marked trees. Areas such as the mature forest of Bush 21 are reserved for research. Often all that the public will notice is someone crouched quietly in the bush writing notes, or a dishevelled figure that bursts out of the bush and rushes ahead to their next study site.

Perhaps Anders Hansen was the first researcher on Tiri. An enthusiastic amateur rather than a trained scientist, his observations express the wonder of a person noticing something for the first time — a desirable trait in any researcher:

> Last Sunday, while looking for plants on a steep, clayey face, I found a plant which was quite new to me. After searching through your book 'Manual of the New Zealand Flora', I came to the conclusion that it must be Drosera auriculata. However, before looking it up in the Flora, I knew I had found one of those curious plants that partly subsist on a flesh diet, if I may call it so. … I potted one of the D. auriculata and planted one in the garden, both were on the point of flowering. The one in the flowerbed has opened its flowers, but the one in the house has not, perhaps because of being shut up in the house. I gave the plant in the house three small pieces of boiled white of egg, which it nearly consumed in 24 hours. I had this plant in the parlour, near a window curtain and a spider (small black one) started to make a web from curtains to cluster of flower buds at top of plant, and had he stopped there things would have been alright for the spider, but he put a stay to the nearest leaf, and that ended his career, for he is now snugly in the centre of the leaf with all the 'feelers' tugged round him. Almost all the leaves had some small insect on them, or rather in them, when I found the plant, and one, a piece of dry stick, blown onto it from a neighbouring pohutukawa, which, however, it had discharged next morning, finding no nourishment therein. So far the plant seems rare here, although I see that you say it is common. (Since found on open grasslands plentifully.)

The sundew (*Drosera*) is not recorded as being on Tiri nowadays, but Daisy Burrell remembers it growing on Whangaparaoa when the peninsula had extensive danthonia grass.

Tiri has amassed a solid body of research over the years. The island is an excellent place to do research: it is a closed system; it is secure — there's no vandalism, and no one is going to build a road through your project two years hence; a researcher can build on the strong body of work already done there; there is a comfortable, convivial place to live; and lastly, Tiri is magic!

John Craig has had many graduate students on Tiri since 1974.[1] The first were Henrick Moller (kiore), Graham Jones (penguins), Terry Bunn (kiore), Mark Dawe (kakariki) and Anne Stewart (tui). Carol West was Neil Mitchell's first botany graduate student in 1978. All were at Auckland University, but nowadays

Facing page: Researcher Matt Low feeds sugar water to a male stitchbird. These hummingbird feeders normally hang in cages that let in stitchbirds and bellbirds but keep out greedy tui.
Matt Low

Tiri has students from many universities.

Researchers may travel back and forth during their research period — Carol West made 24 visits over two years — or may spend months at a time on the island; John Ewen lived in the bunkhouse for several summers, joining Shaun Dunning in his nightly computer games. The bunkhouse provides a comfortable home away from home. The front bedroom is the research room and, thanks to the Supporters' funding and hard work, the kitchen and bathroom facilities are superb — something that is greatly appreciated when researchers stumble in wet, weary and ravenous after a day or night 'in the field'.

When she was studying kiwi, Sibilla Girardet worked from a tent above Pohutukawa Cove. She recalls the storm in March 1995 when 160 millimetres (six inches) of rain fell in just over four hours, and waterspouts formed near Tiri:

Man, that rainstorm was fearsome ... one of those beautiful early spring days ... I was busy cutting a track at the other end of the island when I looked behind me out to sea (toward Little Barrier) and saw this black mass in the distance ... When I next turned around I was just in horror as the bright day was very black and it was closing in fast. I just started running and luckily had my tent close by (in Bush 22)

Fernbird

Fernbird, matata
Bowdleria punctata vealeae
Locally common; endemic.

The Supporters and ARC were the main instigators of the introduction of fernbirds to Tiri. In 2001 a rescue operation was mounted to save fernbirds that were about

to be displaced by the new Northern Motorway near Orewa. Kevin Parker had been monitoring the population, so when scrub clearance began he moved swiftly, assembling a team of helpers, getting DOC to rush through the permit, and obtaining a blessing from Ngati Paoa. Even so, the birds were caught to the roar of approaching bulldozers.

Being fiercely territorial, the birds came to investigate taped calls and flew into a fine mist net. No one was sure how they would cope with the shock of being caught because few transfers of fernbirds had been done before. The first birds caught were rushed to Tiri by helicopter, but later individuals were brought over by ferry. Thirteen were transferred in all. There was little chance of viewing them on release, as they shot out of the box into the depths of the nearest thicket and ... vanished!

From July 2001 to late March 2002, despite diligent searching, Kevin saw only one fernbird. But this individual kept hopes alive for everyone by singing outside the bunkhouse window — most uncharacteristic behaviour for this shy species. This bird had been the first one caught and must have been tough to survive conditions during its capture, such as when the bulldozer driver left his engine running while he wandered over to watch the bird being banded.

In 2002 the sighting of an unbanded fernbird showed that they were already breeding on Tiri, and the fernbird is now established in several areas, particularly around Northeast Valley. Areas of bracken and open scrub are the best places to look and listen for these extremely secretive birds.

Left: A fernbird takes cover on its release on Tiri.
Ian Higgins

and made it just in time before the thunder and lightning started coming down (never mind the rain!). There I sat completely in shock. (I think there had been one lightning strike before I made it into the tent — but what was a tent going to help with, anyway?) ... I'd made a dash for the tent in the late morning ... but then I remember sitting there, keeping myself entertained by writing notes in my field note-book and waiting for the rain to stop when all of a sudden I realised that the heavy rain was NOT going to stop and soon I'd be running out of daylight!!!!! Another panic!

Sibilla abandoned any attempt at tracking kiwi that night and made it back to the bunkhouse before nightfall. The next day the whole island appeared transformed, with small streams having become torrents, washing away everything in their path. 'In Bush 1 there was no leaf litter as far as the eye could see, it was all completely gone. It was like someone had come along with a giant vacuum cleaner and had sucked it all away.' For a while it seemed as if kiwi had been washed away too, for she could not see any of the chicks in their burrows, and one of the kiwi transmitter signals seemed to be coming from out to sea! However, over the next few weeks all the birds were found to be safe.

The bunkhouse, formerly a lighthouse keeper's house, on the slope facing Auckland. Matt Low

Below left: The bunkhouse provides a home away from home for researchers: the bustle in the bunkhouse kitchen. Anne Rimmer

It is not surprising that several romances and marriages began on Tiri: John Craig, lecturer, and Ann Stewart, PhD student, were married in 1984; Jason Taylor, DOC contractor, and Shaarina Boyd, protected species officer, married in 2000; and in 2002, Graham Ussher, ARC herpetologist, and Ruby Jones, restoration ecologist, were married on the island.

The bunkhouse has a constantly changing mix of people, which yields lively conversations at mealtimes. As well as the students, there may be DOC contractors, visiting scientists, bird watchers, Supporters on the island as guides, builders or workers, casual volunteers staying a week or more, a weekend group from a tramping club or Forest and Bird and — if there's room — members of the general public, including overseas visitors. Information is shared readily, with probably the most frequently asked question being: where is the best place to see kiwi?

It's not only birds that are studied: insects, weeds, kiore, even the visitors have been examined. In research, things sometimes go wrong. Little spotted kiwi were fitted with transmitters when they were introduced in 1993. One bird died when its harness got caught on a bush; the others were immediately caught to remove their harnesses, and new transmitters were fitted later. Researchers are often at the whim of the weather: good weather may cause birds to nest early, before the researcher has arrived. And their hours are dictated by their subjects: those who band petrels, track kiwi or chase penguins must be nocturnal.

In a novel use of GPS (Global Positioning System), penguins were caught, fitted with a small GPS and sent off to sea. When they could be caught again, which isn't easy (researchers of penguins being recognisable by their skinned knees and bitten hands), the GPS showed the penguins' travels.

Both DOC and the Supporters fund some research: each of the endangered birds was intensively studied. Supporters enjoy helping by making bird observations, collecting seed, etc. Some work is tedious: Carol West, collecting seeds from seed traps, counted 8633 kanuka, 19,333 manuka and 1516 pohutukawa seeds — all tiny seeds.

Ray and Barbara Walter have contributed a huge body of observations. 'Ray knows when his birds turn right and when they turn left.' Their 'Flora and Fauna' notes in the *Dawn Chorus* comprise an excellent record. Graham Ussher pays tribute to them:

Ray and Barbara have always been eager to share their knowledge with others. When I arrived on the island that first August [1990], I was in the middle of a botanical course at university and was having a lot of trouble discriminating between various New Zealand native plants. Barbara spent a whole day with me around different parts of the island showing me plants and specimen trees and giving me hints to tell them apart. Ray then spent hours in the nursery showing me young trees and imparting his years of knowledge. I will never forget the generosity and patience that they showed.

Banding and naming

Banding (bird identification by coloured leg bands) follows an international code. A numbered metal band (M) and coloured plastic bands, e.g. Red (R), etc. are fitted on the legs. The colours are read: left leg, top to bottom, right leg, top to bottom. Thus the kokako Te Koha Waiata is YG/RM.

Banding is usually done before the chicks fledge (leave the nest) and the bands remain on for life. One evening a group was practising banding in the Tiri bunkhouse. They used dry spaghetti, knowing that if they broke the spaghetti, they would probably break a bird's leg.

On Tiri, all the takahe, kokako, hihi, robins, some fernbirds and some older saddlebacks are banded.

The takahe are all named. Some names are chosen by DOC workers; others come from contests among Supporters. Some are inspired by appearance — Opal, Sapphire, Pounamu (greenstone); some are mellifluous Maori (Aroha, Iti, Whetu) and some are named after something or someone (Bellamy, Greg, Kristin).

The kokako are also named. There are musical terms (Piccolo and Bel Canto), Kanuka after the tree he hatched in and, in 2004, Keisha after the young star of the New Zealand film *Whale Rider*.

Most other species are too numerous for individual naming, although a friendly robin on the Wattle Track was dubbed Christmas because its leg bands were red and green.

This male stitchbird is banded RM/G, a unique identification. Peter Craw

~

FIFTEEN

FRUITION

The past 10 years has been a time of growth and maturation for Tiritiri Matangi — both in its natural habitat and for the organisations that tend the island.

In 2004 it was:

33 years since Tiri was made a reserve;

30 years since the kakariki tempted John Craig to investigate the island;

24 years since Ray Walter arrived;

20 years since the planting programme began;

15 years since the Supporters of Tiritiri Matangi was founded;

10 years since planting ended.

As the tree-planting period ended, school visits increased, with many schools bringing multiple classes and returning every year. Fifty-four schools visited in the past year. Most children are well prepared and gain a good overview of conservation principles while enjoying their day on Tiri. They are given a guided tour, reaching the lighthouse in time for lunch.

A Fullers ferry comes three days a week in winter, and almost daily in the summer, with many trips being fully booked. The trip takes 30 minutes from Auckland to Gulf Harbour and 15 minutes across to Tiri. The size and safety of the Fullers fleet means that few trips are cancelled because of bad weather.

Visitor numbers have grown by about 10 percent each year. The daily limit for people arriving on commercial boats is 150, with no limit on those who land from private boats. In 2003, 33,261 people visited the island.

But visitor numbers for January 2004 shot up 20 percent. There were 6032 visitors that month, of which 916 were from overseas, and about 2335 from private boats. Over $9000 was taken in guiding fees and the shop took almost $31,000 — that's $1000 a day. The Supporters' total income in 2003 was $266,767.

Surveys have shown that visitor satisfaction is very high on Tiri, with 98 percent of visitors being very satisfied with their

Girls from Trident High School, Whakatane, find sandhoppers for Greg, @dot, and their chick, Tiri. Such close encounters with endangered birds embody the magic of the island. Anne Rimmer

Rain! Ray Walter with visitors. Anne Rimmer

The former potting shed and tiny shop are often crowded at lunchtime. Eve Manning

Far right: Barbara Walter guides a group of schoolchildren. Roving Tortoise Photos

experience. There are increasing numbers of overseas visitors — Tiri is listed in the *Lonely Planet Guide to New Zealand* — while others hear of the island by word of mouth. There is a need for a foreign-language leaflet to explain the rules of the island. With New Zealand being Lonely Planet's top destination for two years running, and the success of films such as *The Lord of the Rings* and *Whale Rider*, tourism is a rapidly growing industry for the whole country.

One gets used to seeing famous people on Tiri: Prime Minister Helen Clark brought Australian Prime Minister John Howard over by helicopter for a two-hour break in 2001; Jeanette Fitzsimons, co-leader of the Green Party, comes with her local Forest and Bird branch; prominent businessmen like Michael Hill dropped by during the America's Cup; and Canadian author Margaret Atwood has visited.

At lunchtime, the shop is a busy place, as visitors and their bulky backpacks cram into the tiny room. Kerry Teague's hand-painted T-shirts were the first items for sale back in 1986, and demand still outstrips supply. No food is sold, but complimentary tea and coffee are available. It is unusual to find a commercial enterprise in a DOC reserve, and until 1998 the shop's takings went into 'DOC's big milk bucket', as Ray and Barbara put it. Now that the Supporters have the shop concession, all profit is returned to the island. This tiny emporium made $49,139 in 2003.

The lack of proper visitor facilities on Tiri is most worrisome in bad weather. On fine days, visitors spread out over the whole lighthouse area, but when it rains everyone must huddle in the potting shed and the garage. And Tiri has recently endured some of the wettest winters Ray has experienced in his 24 years on the island. Worst is the inability to protect the schoolchildren, some of whom are woefully underdressed and shivering after a wet walk up to the lighthouse area.

The sorry saga of the non-existent visitor centre is one of the few negatives in the Tiri story. Michael Cole drew up a design 20 years ago and Ray wrote in 1989, 'It is very important that a final plan for the proposed implement shed, visitor centre, toilets etc. ... be drawn up.' John Hawley, a well-respected DOC planner, produced a pleasing design that got nowhere; then DOC commissioned a design from the architect Harry Turbott in 1994. Turbott's design had several features that the Supporters felt were inappropriate for Tiri: at two-thirds the height of the

Left: Current DOC officer
Ian Price in the well-
equipped implement
shed. Anne Rimmer

lighthouse, the building would have dominated the historic lighthouse compound, and the building 'looked to the lighthouse' — a man-made object — rather than looking out onto the newly planted forest. To make matters worse, DOC proposed to build the structure from a confiscated shipment of Chilean hardwood — a protected rainforest species.

The Supporters then put forward their own design but nothing came of that either. It remains Ray Walter's greatest wish to have the visitor centre built. The Supporters' committee has recently obtained DOC's approval and all the required permits for a new set of plans. Now only finance is needed.

While Tiri has fewer visitors than, for example, the National Parks, an island has special needs. If the weather worsens, or someone feels ill, they can't go home early, or retreat to their car as they could do on the mainland. As well, high-profile Tiri, with

The curious case of the kakariki on the flax

Tall flax plants grow over much of the island. This has surprised everyone because flax did not show up as a potential colonising species in Carol West's study nor in the HGMP management plan of 1982. Flax normally favours damp conditions but has adapted well to Tiri's dry climate.

Flax provides nectar for the honeyeaters and seeds for kakariki and others, and birds with orange pollen-dusted heads are common in the flax-flowering season. Flax also shelters penguins and kiwi.

In the late 1990s, the kakariki on Tiri developed a taste for the soft green flowerbuds of the flax. They ate vast quantities of the flowers, destroying a valuable nectar source for the honeyeaters and preventing any seeds developing. This situation prevailed for three years. In 2000 only two flax-flower stems survived on the whole island and the situation was little better the following year. Had another nectar source, such as the kowhai, also failed or been late or early in flowering, the food shortage might have been dire for the three nectar-eating species: tui, bellbird and hihi.

However, in a typical boom-and-bust cycle, kakariki numbers dropped significantly over the winter of 2001, and in the next two years the flax flowering was outstanding. Whether the kakariki population fell because of deaths over the winter when food is traditionally scarce, or whether many birds left the island is not known.

A kakariki perches on chewed flax-flower stems.
Eve Manning

its many overseas visitors, should be regarded as a flagship location and given the gold-star treatment.

While the visitor centre remained on the drawing board, other structures were being built. The service facility/implement shed (aka 'Ray's Shed') was funded and built by the Supporters over a four-year period, with generous donations from many organisations. Doing work of this scale on an island can be complicated: pouring concrete for a shed floor involved 'four barge trips, and the landing of six concrete trucks'. The complex was completed in 2002 at a cost of $170,000. It houses the vehicles and mechanical equipment, which need protection from Tiri's salt-laden winds.

The wharf shelter, erected in 2003, is a particularly graceful design that, curving round a large cabbage tree, already looks as if it has been there forever. It will soon have display boards telling the island's story.

The wharf shelter: Greg greets the author.
Barbara Hughes

RECREATIONAL BOATING

A surprising number of recreational boaties are still not aware that they do not need a permit to land on Tiri. Nevertheless, there were 75 boats anchored off Hobbs Beach on Auckland Anniversary weekend 2004, and the beach was crowded. Many boaties go no further than the beach, or opt for a swift constitutional up to the lighthouse. They are generous in leaving donations in the box. Private boats are not counted in the daily limit of 150 people. Those who anchor overnight (advisable only in calm, easterly conditions) are rewarded with kiwi calls at night, and the best dawn chorus in New Zealand.

Large crowds were expected at Tiri during the first America's Cup yacht races in 2000. DOC considered closing the island, but instead added two extra staff. The Supporters also increased their presence on the island (from which they had an excellent view of the racing), but no mishaps occurred at all. Things were consequently more relaxed for the second America's Cup in 2003, though it was a bit of a shock when spectator boats containing 400 people decided to head for Tiri after a weekend race was cancelled. Hobbs Beach was crowded, and the shop on Tiri did a brisk trade that day!

There is always the risk of a careless boatie letting a cat or dog loose on the island or starting a fire by smoking in the dry grass behind the beach. But recreational boaties are generally self-regulating. Many of them care passionately about Tiri, and are swift to correct others who do not observe the rules.

Soon after Ray Walter came to Tiri, he was shocked to see smoke rising from Hobbs Beach one morning. Hurrying down, he found a group of marathon swimmers having a barbecue. The tradition had started in the mid-1970s when the Cook Strait swimmer Perry Cameron took seven hours to swim from Tiri to Mairangi Bay, as a fundraiser for the Mairangi Bay Surf Lifesaving Club.

Many people enjoy a swim at Hobbs Beach. An added thrill comes from finding that one is sharing the clear water with a ray

(the unbearded sort). When orca were feeding off Tiri, the author counted eight rays in ankle-deep water, and large stingrays and eagle rays can often be seen beneath the wharf.

Seals have only rarely been reported but dolphins and whales are increasing in the Gulf. During the Queen's Birthday working weekend in 2001, dolphins put on a magnificent display at Hobbs Beach.

Kayakers favour the eastern side of Tiri: 'The Far Side is adorned with high cliffs, spectacular sea caves and a myriad rock gardens — enough to test anyone's paddling ability and nerve. … The Arches is an area about halfway down the island worth exploring, as are the caves at the southern end.'[1] One guide, Dianne Michels, is a keen kayaker who sometimes paddles over 'to work'. She arrived one weekend with a group that had paddled from Motuora Island in choppy conditions.

Fishermans Bay and Shearer Rock are popular anchorages for fishing, though fish catches have declined markedly in recent years.

Divers favour the rocky northern end of the island, where they can catch crayfish. Roger Grace, a marine biologist, recalls his first trip to Tiri:

… I enjoyed a wonderful day snorkelling at Little Wooded Island and in Northeast Bay. This was probably in the summer of 1960–61.

The underwater visibility on that day was about 70 feet, or just over 20 metres! Ecklonia kelp covered most of the rocky bottom. Red crayfish feelers bristled from beneath ledges and rocks. I was 15, and used a thick woollen jersey to help keep me warm, as wetsuits were just in their infancy then. … Several keen spear fishermen used to spear kingfish on the bottom using scuba gear … huge kingfish, sometimes in excess of 50 pounds (23 kilograms).

Jenny and Tony Enderby, natural history photojournalists stationed at Leigh, are also Tiri guides. They too have been documenting and writing about the island's marine life for a long time.

School tours usually stop at the beach before catching the ferry, and the intertidal areas are an excellent teaching resource. (Notably, there are no mangroves, because there are no mud-flats.) The reserve goes right down to the low-water mark, and Ray cautions children to replace every rock they turn over on the beach, 'and you adults, no throwing our lovely round stones back into the ocean'. Some overseas visitors do not even know that tides exist, and overseas students, through ignorance, can be destructive in the rock pools.

Algal blooms sometimes appear, forming large opaque plumes like spilled pink paint. The organisms are bioluminescent. When collected, the water is thick and sago-like.

The proposal for a marine reserve, put forward in 2002 by the New Zealand Underwater Association and Forest and Bird, has proved controversial, with recreational fishermen mounting an organised opposition. The Tiri Supporters' committee has endeavoured to stand aside from the debate, fearing it might politicise their membership.

The Cave Creek disaster in 1995 in which a DOC viewing platform collapsed — killing 14 young people and severely injuring four more — was a major wake-up call for the department and has affected many of its decisions since. In the wake of this tragedy, any potentially unsafe structure under DOC's control was closed until it could be inspected, and either certified safe or modified.

DOC closed Tiri's wharf on 2 May 1995, two days after Cave Creek. The old structure had been scheduled for replacement for some time, but DOC had no finance available for the work. With the cancellation of all the ferry trips, the wharf's closure caused major inconvenience and financial hardship for the island. Following emergency repairs, the wharf reopened on 19 May.

After many delays, a larger concrete wharf was finally built in 1998. Ray used timbers from the old wharf to build four sturdy bridges, dubbed 'tank crossings', on the Eastern Track,

which easily met DOC's new safety regulations.

The wharf can be unsafe in windy conditions. There is an emergency landing area on the east coast and on one occasion visitors, including a number of older American women, had to be carried out piggyback style to a rowboat in order to reach the ferry. When high winds in 1998 prevented the ferry from docking, 64 people were evacuated by two helicopters.

The viewing platform where the Wattle Track meets the road carries one of the bird identification signs put up by the Supporters. This is a popular place to sit in the hope that a kokako may appear, or at least sing nearby. The kokako, introduced in 1997, and still few in number, is the bird that most visitors long to see when they come to Tiri — and the one that gives them most joy when they succeed. (See Chapter 17, 'Kokako — the Gift of Song'.)

Building a composting toilet at Hobbs Beach, installing water tanks, cutting tracks, pouring concrete, digging dams: an island's work … Much of this work is done on Supporters' working weekends when — inspired by Ray — the unfit, the elderly and small children alike undertake manual labour they would regard as completely beyond them on the mainland. Gael Arnold has

'Framed'. Members of the Supporters building the implement shed. From left: Kevin Barker, Val Smytheman, Trevor Buckley, Peter Lee, Katherine Danaher, Simon Fordham, Marilyn Buckley, Barbara Hughes, Dennis Green, Sally Green, John Turner. Anon.

Bipedicus enormous

In 1994, Ray was host to a group of 16 members of the American Lighthouse Association. While standing speaking to the group, in his shorts, Ray was interrupted by one of the women members of the party who asked if he had developed his strong legs walking up all those lighthouse steps. After reflecting for a moment, Ray replied that he probably had, whereupon the visitor, impressed, took a photo of the memorable pair of 'bipeds'.

Ray on his new 'moa'. Carl Hayson

brought a group over for 14 years. Louise and David Gauld's group has been coming for a similar time. Louise articulates what so many volunteers feel: 'each small task contributes to the most wonderful communal project I have ever had the privilege to be part of. I think everyone who works there feels "woven" into the place — especially as the warm welcome from Ray and Barbara makes one feel like part of a family.'

Against the wishes of the Supporters, DOC gave Telecom permission to put up a cellphone tower on Tiri for the 2000 America's Cup. Peter Lee, who took over from Mel Galbraith as chair of the Supporters, was vocal in his opposition. One 'benefit' from this intrusion was that Telecom upgraded the road, laying red chip, which may be a tough surface but is annoyingly crunchy underfoot when one is trying to creep around at night in search of kiwi.

In the lighthouse area, some restoration is under way. DOC commissioned a survey in 1997 that documented the historic value of the lighthouse and its surrounding buildings. The signal tower has been partly restored and the diaphonic foghorn building strengthened. Carl Hayson, the past chairman of the Supporters, is the driving force in this restoration work.

The lighthouse itself is showing some rust, which distresses ex-lighthouse keepers when they see it (see photo on page 56), but it looks fit to stand a few more years. Thus it is particularly galling that the lighthouse, closed 'on safety grounds' in 1995, remains firmly shut today. Even Ray, the last lighthouse keeper, is forbidden entry.

As the workload increased, more vehicles have been needed on the island. The Supporters have funded a new ute, quad, tractor and 'moa'.[2]

In 1998 the Supporters won the Loder Cup, a prestigious Conservation Award. The cup is inscribed: 'Offered to lovers of nature in New Zealand to encourage the protection and cultivation of the incomparable flora and fauna of the dominion'. It was presented to the Supporters in a ceremony on board the *Hauturu* by the Minister of Conservation, Nick Smith, who said:

A working bee making a new accessway to Hobbs Beach. Anne Rimmer

Above left: The lighthouse station from Coronary Hill (cf. page 41, the same view in 1912). Anne Rimmer

Mel Galbraith and friend with the Loder Cup.
Mel Galbraith

Right: The author guiding Kelston Primary School children. The bird-identification sign behind was provided by the Supporters. Geoff Keen

This habitat has been created by members of the community freely giving their time and energy under the guidance of a partnership between the Supporters and the Department [of Conservation]. . . . The award . . . acknowledges the contribution of many thousands of people from all walks of life who helped make this project such an outstanding success.

As a fundraiser in 2000, the Supporters arranged a private showing of the Imax 3D movie on the Galapagos Islands. Six hundred and sixty people attended, raising $2500. Other novel fundraising has included a ballot for the right to release a brown teal in 1990, ENZA's Apple Crunch Day for schoolchildren which gave the island $11,000 in 1993, and David Bellamy's speech in 1999 at a British Airways' function in London. Displaying a huge NativeZ takahe toy, he explained about Tiri and invited donations from his audience.[3] This delightful gesture raised $2000.

The current chair of the Supporters, Simon Fordham, set up the Tiri website in 1998 and has been an editor of the newsletter, which was renamed the *Dawn Chorus* in 2001. From its modest one-sheet beginnings in 1989, Tiri's quarterly bulletin has grown to a 12-page full-colour publication. Many of the photos in this book were first published in the *Dawn Chorus*.

The Supporters of Tiritiri Matangi Inc. is now one of the largest conservation groups in New Zealand, with membership exceeding 1400. As well as receiving the newsletters, members can attend special events and lectures, and non-working or working weekends on Tiri. Since the bunkhouse is in such high demand, an organised weekend is often the only way to be able to stay on the island.

Water can be scarce: people are sometimes asked to bring water with them, and short showers are a must. The addition of the catchment area on the implement shed, along with eight huge tanks (22,000-litre capacity) now helps the water situation. Drinking water is now sterilised by an ultraviolet system.

The guided tours have rapidly become a major source of income. Originally Barbara and Ray did all of the guiding, often of large groups; the $2 fee went to DOC. Barbara regularly

guided school groups of 45 children. When Fullers introduced bigger boats, a more formal guiding system was needed.

The first guiding meeting was held in 1999 with 50 guides. There were over 140 guides in 2004, with still more needed. The $5 fee now goes directly to the island and guiding made $36,360 in 2003. Simon Fordham was the original guiding coordinator, followed by Sally Green. A comprehensive 'Guiding Manual' supplies the information needed for the guides to give a 90-minute to 2-hour tour. (This information is also on the Tiri website: www.tiritirimatangi.org.nz.) A thirst for knowledge has led to regular evening meetings where guides learn more about tree identification, birds, bats, weeds, etc. The speaker is usually the primary researcher or a Supporter with special knowledge of the subject. A first-aid course is taught regularly by Liz Maire, a guide and an outdoor instructor, and the guides carry a bag with emergency supplies. Weekly emails keep guides up to date. They contain information on practical matters like track closures and safety concerns, and an update on flora and fauna.

Barbara Walter coordinates the guiding. With her usual efficiency she staffs the phone at 7 am each day, for the day's guides to check in. Since 2000, Fullers Ferries has carried guides for free, saving the island over $10,000 per year.

While most guides come over just for the day, some volunteers stay on the island to work, or to help run things while Ray and Barbara are on leave. Ian Higgins has put in months of carpentry work, while Yvonne Vaneveld and Mike Siddons calculated that one year they had spent more time on Tiri than in their own home. Yvonne is one of a rostered group who organise the guiding when Barbara is away. Val Smytheman is another dedicated volunteer, and the time she has spent on Tiri has enabled her to take some of the photographs for this book. Another of the photographers, Peter Craw, has spent two summers working on the weed team.

While this chapter is more about 'plant' in the industrial sense than about 'plants' in the botanical sense, on Tiri one never forgets the plants and birds that are the island's raison d'être. The introduction of the stitchbird to Tiri in 1995 required careful preparation because several previous translocations of stitchbirds had failed.

In a move that fully met Tiri's ideals, Shaarina Boyd, DOC protected species officer, invited Mel Galbraith's pupils at

Glenfield College to be part of the transfer process. They wrote the official translocation project, built and installed special nest boxes and feeding stations, researched food resources and then planted 100 extra gloxinia plants, and even designed the project's logo. It is not surprising that some of these students have gone on to careers in conservation.

Thirteen students spent a fortnight on Little Barrier Island helping to catch the birds, and others were at the public release on Tiri. Little Barrier tangata whenua, Ngati Wai, handed the birds into the care of Tiritiri guardians, the Kawerau and Ngati Paoa tribes. The hihi were released at three sites, watched by groups of spectators. 'Enthusiastic comments were made by those at the release sites as to how well they had been able to view the birds and their sense of involvement in the occasion.'

Thanks to careful monitoring and intervention by a dedicated team, particularly Jason Taylor and John Ewen in the early stages, the population has grown rapidly. Whereas one felt privileged to see a stitchbird only a few years ago, they are now common. Some are almost too tame: in 2003 a young man arrived at the shop claiming that a stitchbird had landed on his finger. When doubt was expressed, he triumphantly produced the evidence on his digital camera.

The special stitchbird feeders, incorporating a hummingbird feeder, keep the syrup clean — thus minimising the spread of disease. Chelsea Sugar donates over a ton of sugar a year: 'Something to really sing about' as they chirruped in a recent advertisement.

When Graham Ussher and Ruby Jones were married on the island in 2002, even the birds celebrated, with a New Zealand dotterel flying over, calling, during the ceremony.

The culmination of years of hard work, especially by Graham Ussher, occurred in 2003, when tuatara were reintroduced to Tiri. The public release at Labour Weekend was an emotional event for many of the 300 attending. After the tuatara had been blessed by iwi, Graham and the other handlers took them among the crowd where people reached out to stroke the large, passive reptiles. (See Tuatara box in Chapter 13, 'The Non-birds'.)

'Ladies and Gentlemen! Welcome to Tiritiri Matangi. My name is Ray Walter, and this is my wife Barbara …' Ray Walter gives his introductory talk. Anne Rimmer

Left: Mr Blue checks up on Mel Galbraith and Glenfield College pupils building stitchbird nesting boxes. Zane Burdett

The Supporters organised and paid for the release, which cost $6834, with financial assistance coming from the Tindall Foundation and others. Tuatara were listed in Tiri's original 1982 working plan, though only for release on Little Wooded Island, since Tiri itself still had kiore on it at that stage. Approval from DOC's tuatara recovery group was granted in 1999. Graham Ussher comments that the length of time that the translocation took from its inception to completion (five years) demonstrates the amount of planning and consultation required.

The bare area south of the lighthouse has recently been planted as takahe habitat: open meadows with clumps of shrubs for the birds to take shelter in. This has meant renewed activity in the nursery, with pleasing rows of different species growing there. Visitors can buy trees.

Ralph Silvester, whose association with Tiri stretches back 20 years, donated funds for the establishment of a wetland area to improve conditions for the brown teal. After extensive consultation with DOC on the design and location, heavy earth-moving equipment arrived by barge in autumn 2003, but an exceptionally wet winter slowed progress badly. Comments on

Stitchbird

Stitchbird, hihi
Notiomystis cincta
Protected; threatened; endemic.

Since disappearing from the mainland in the 1800s, stitchbirds were found only on Little Barrier Island. Previous transfers to other islands have failed (Hen, Cuvier and Mokoia Islands) or not thrived as expected (Kapiti Island).

DuPont funded the transfer of 37 stitchbirds (19 male, 18 female) from Little Barrier Island on 3 September 1995. The birds were released at three sites: in Bush 1, Wattle Valley and Bush 22. Only 17 birds survived the stress of transfer, but even so, six chicks were raised in that first season. However, from a second transfer on 27 August 1996 only two out of 13 birds survived to breed.

Despite this shaky beginning the Tiri population has grown well, and by spring 2003 there were 109 adult birds living in many parts of the island. Pairs commonly raise two broods of chicks per season (with up to five chicks in each) and more nesting boxes have been put up to accommodate the rapidly growing population. These boxes are needed as the forest on Tiri currently does not provide enough natural nesting holes. The boxes also allow nest monitoring and treatment of parasites that may kill nestlings.

The first nest in a natural cavity was found in a pohutukawa in 2002. 'Natural' nestings will increase as the regenerating forest matures and more holes suitable for nesting appear.

Stitchbirds are unique in the bird world, in that as well as mating in the typical bird position (male standing on the female's back), they can also mate face-to-face, with the female on her back and the male lying on top. Dr Matt Low, who is also a vet, has shown that face-to-face mating is a forced copulation (or 'rape'), where females struggle to prevent males from mating with them.

Tiri's success with the stitchbird means that DOC's stitchbird recovery group is now considering using Tiri birds to start new populations elsewhere. Ongoing research and the intensive management of the birds on Tiri are helping to ensure that this species has a future.

A female stitchbird. Anne Rimmer

Matt Low checks a stitchbird nesting box. Matt Low

Not a honeyeater

Recent DNA evidence suggests that the stitchbird is not a member of the honeyeater family (which contains bellbirds and tui) as had been supposed, but ... something else. Research by John Ewen in France may reveal what group the stitchbird should belong to.

the absurdity of rain preventing the creation of a wetland were rife.

The rain also made tracks treacherously slippery that winter, and urgent upgrading was done after several people suffered broken bones. Fortunately, accidents are not common on the island. One exception was when Mel Galbraith fell down the cliffs above Hobbs Beach in 1995. He was banding petrels at night with his teenage daughter Maria when the ground gave way beneath him. He landed on rocks below, sustaining severe injuries. As he crawled around, semi-conscious, penguins jumped over him.

Maria was reluctant to leave her father to go for help. Most unusually, but fortunately for Mel, a couple from a boat had come ashore, and they raised the alarm. The helicopter landed at 1 am on Coronary Hill, which is kept mown for this purpose. Mel spent 10 days in hospital.

It is heartening that there has been a major improvement in relations between the Supporters and DOC administration in the past few years (there have always been excellent relations with DOC field workers, who are highly regarded). DOC now treats the Supporters more as partners, and the Supporters are left to run the island in consultation with DOC. Rob McCallum, the present conservator for Auckland, says:

> The model provided by the Tiritiri project, where a central government agency has joined forces with a community-based conservation group, has proved a highly successful one. There have been important lessons to both parties that can now be exported to other areas of New Zealand, and indeed the world. Whilst some lessons have been specific to Tiritiri, others are more generic, including those pertaining to governance structures, financial management, fund-raising mechanisms, strategic planning and volunteer mobilisation and management.

Throughout this project there has been a remarkable continuity of the people involved: John Craig has been involved for 30 years, and Neil Mitchell for 27; Ray Walter arrived on Tiri 24 years ago, and Barbara Walter 19 years ago; the Galbraith family

The nursery today, growing trees for the takahe meadows.
Anne Rimmer

Left: A powhiri (welcome) for the stitchbirds in 1995.
Zane Burdett

Far left: Ruby Jones, Ray Walter, Mel Galbraith and Graham Ussher in 1995.
Zane Burdett

123

have been coming for 21 years, Elizabeth Morton for 20, and Carl Hayson for 16; Jim Battersby, founder of the Supporters 16 years ago, is now a guide; and Graham Ussher has had various roles over 14 years. This continuity has facilitated research for this book because the key people are still available and involved.

As is common in volunteer groups, many of Tiri's guides are middle-aged, but an encouraging number of younger people are becoming involved. Some researchers who have grown to love Tiri become guides to continue their association with the island.

It is heartening to see a second generation of Supporters and guides. Ian McLeod first came tree-planting at the age of three, with his parents Kay and John, who are still very active in the

Supporters; Ian was a DOC officer on the island from 2000 to 2002. His successor, Ian Price, is also a Supporter.

Mel and Sonia Galbraith, and three of their daughters, are now guides, as is their daughter Sarah's husband, Andrew Williams. Sarah and Andrew's baby son Oskar is a third-generation Tiri Supporter. His grandfather Mel says, 'None of us ever envisaged being at the point we are now. Tiri has been an innovation, sociologically and scientifically.'

Frank Arnott, a former secretary of the HGMP Board, said in 1983, 'At the end of the century there will still be things to do.' He was correct, but at the Tiri reunion in 2003 he was able to see how much has already been achieved.

One of the last photos taken (in 1992) from the lighthouse before it was closed in 1995. Pat Greenfield

Ray and Barbara QSM

In the New Year's Honours of 2002, Ray and Barbara Walter were awarded the Queen's Service Medal for Public Service, an honour they richly deserved. The *Dawn Chorus* paid tribute to their contribution thus: 'They truly are the face of Tiri, meeting, greeting, making people feel special and bringing alive the joy of conservation.'

Pat Greenfield

Tiri reunion

On 9 November 2003, 130 people with links to Tiri came back for a reunion. The event was organised by the author to thank those who had contributed to this book.

The group included ex-lighthouse keepers and their families, some dating back to the 1920s, members of the Hauraki Gulf Maritime Park Board from the 1970s and 1980s, University of Auckland staff who spear-headed the replanting programme from 1984 to 1994, early researchers, many members of the Supporters of Tiritiri Matangi Inc., members of the Hobbs family who farmed Tiri from the early 1900s, DOC and ARC scientists and administrators, volunteers and tree planters.

Ray and Barbara Walter were delighted to see so many old friends. It was a glorious sunny day and everyone enjoyed the gathering. A dinner that evening was attended by 60 people, including Darcy O'Brien and Graham Turbott, who were key people at the beginning of the Tiri Conservation Project.

2003 reunion. Gordon Ell

~

SIXTEEN

TAKAHE — AMBASSADORS FOR THE ENDANGERED

Takahe
Porphyrio hochstetteri
Protected; endangered; endemic.

Takahe are birds back from the brink. Thought to have become extinct by the late nineteenth century, they were rediscovered in 1948 by Dr Geoffrey Orbell, an Invercargill doctor who was a keen deer-hunter. The small population of about 250–300 birds was living high up near the snowline in an isolated part of Fiordland.[1] The rediscovery of the *Notornis,* as they were then called, was a world sensation. 'It was the best thing for NZ since the end of the war.'[2] But, although a 500-square-kilometre special area was immediately set aside for them, the population dwindled, and it was decided to try to raise birds in captivity.

Gerald Durrell's description in *Two in the Bush* — of carrying takahe eggs out from the Murchison Mountains under a bantam hen — is hilarious and substantially true, according to Dave Crouchley of DOC's takahe recovery team. Because the precious eggs had to be kept warm while being transported, a group of bantam hens was put through a mini-commando course to find the hen least likely to panic and desert her post while being jolted down the rugged terrain of Fiordland. The 'survivor' was the bantam whose box was accidentally knocked off the top of a car, and was found upside down on the road after having rolled several times. When the box was opened they found a very grim bantam still doggedly brooding her dummy egg.

It took many years before the takahe captive-breeding

Blending in: a Tiri takahe finds a friend. Pat Greenfield

Facing page: Mr Blue's ablutions. Pat Greenfield

There are still only about 240 takahe in total, and Tiri is home to about 18 of them.

Right: As near as takahe
get to flying. Matt Low

programme was successful, but takahe are now routinely bred in captivity at Burwood Bush, Te Anau, and small populations are safely established in several locations throughout New Zealand, including on predator-free offshore islands such as Tiritiri Matangi. DOC's takahe recovery programme manages the populations to maintain as much genetic diversity as possible. Chicks bred at Burwood are taken back to the mountains.

The first two takahe arrived on Tiri from Maud Island on 28 May 1991. Stormy had hatched on Maud, while Mr Blue hatched at Te Anau on 12 December 1984 from one of the 'wild' eggs that were carried out. He was later transferred to Maud Island. The new arrivals settled in well and stayed mainly around the lighthouse area — to the relief of Barbara Walter, who had worried how she would keep tabs on her precious charges if they vanished to the far ends of the island.

When these two male birds repeatedly built nests they were given an egg, flown at great effort from Maud Island. Four days later the chick hatched, and was named Matangi. Her devoted foster parents, both bird and human, successfully raised her, even when, at a few days old, she was found wet and cold standing in

Mel Galbraith and Ray Walter carry the precious takahe egg, flown from Maud Island, 1992. Anon.

a puddle after a torrential downpour. The sodden baby was dried with a hairdryer and put into the shed with Mr Blue, who arranged grass (hastily collected and also dried with the hairdryer) into a nest for the night. People took turns sitting up all night to drive off any kiore that might attack.

'In true Plunket fashion', Matangi was weighed weekly. She grew almost to adulthood but, sadly, died at 10 months.

However, by then JJ, an adult female, had been brought to Tiri. She soon paired with Stormy (who happened to be her uncle) and the pair parented many of the takahe hatched on Tiri.

The first captive-reared takahe had been raised by hand, and were thus at ease with people; Mr Blue was one of these. On Tiri, he strolled through the houses, climbed onto the lap of anyone who would have him, wrestled with shoelaces and begged food shamelessly. Children adored him.

Mr Blue's life went downhill as he aged, and after a series of mishaps, some requiring urgent helicopter trips to Auckland Zoo for vet treatment, Mr Blue died on 28 November 1996, aged twelve. Though he was on Tiri for only five years, his impact was enormous. Mr Blue is buried beneath a puriri tree on the lawn below the lighthouse, where his obituary plaque reads in part: '... he generated a warmth in the hearts and minds of all who were privileged to meet him'.

Takahe have reached over 20 years of age in captivity, but 15 is more likely for a wild bird. They do not always mate for life, and the Tiri population (around the lighthouse area in particular), is in a constant state of flux, the matchings and break-ups rivalling 'Shortland Street', New Zealand's long-running TV soap opera. Regrettably, a battle in 2002 resulted in the death of a chick. Such incidents are distressing and frustrating. Barbara Walter says it's a pity takahe can't read — to learn how endangered they are.

Barbara is the only person allowed to feed them, and 'the Tarks', as they are known, jump to attention whenever she appears, trotting determinedly after her as she goes about her busy day. If she is off the island, they mope like abandoned pets. They are so attached to people that they also run after the three vehicles on the island. In a unique and tragic statistic, a female takahe, Opal, was killed when she ran out in front of the quad bike — surely the only takahe ever to be killed by a motorised vehicle.

Takahe have a frustratingly low breeding rate, with a high incidence of infertile eggs and a high chick mortality. A newly hatched chick is a fluffy black ball with a white egg tooth on the tip of its beak. This is used for chipping itself out of its shell, an exercise which can take days. The little chick stays well hidden in the undergrowth and is fed insects by its parents. Older siblings also help, and one chick, Blakie, grew fat with four adult relatives feeding him. (Blakie hatched soon after yachtsman Sir Peter Blake's death and wears red bands in memory of Sir Peter's red socks.)

Takahe can be careless of their offspring: one family group hatched two chicks in 2000. A few days later they went for a walk in Wattle Valley and 'lost' one — perhaps takahe are unable to count beyond one?

More children wrote to the New Zealand Herald *after Mr Blue's death than on any other topic in the history of the newspaper.*

Left: JJ establishes the pecking order with Ray Walter on arrival, 1992. *New Zealand Herald*

Parental care: @dot and Greg with their chick, Tiri, 2003. Val Smytheman

Blakie shows his disapproval of the sign's message. Jonathan Higgins

Above right: A takahe going about its business. Anne Mein

Greg is the only bird to have been branded an OSH hazard!

The feather and leg colours develop gradually in a chick's first year, while the family remains as a group. If a takahe becomes separated it sets up a loud, raucous, two-note rising call, with others joining in until the family is reunited. A contented takahe will utter soft cooing noises. Their other sound is a deep 'boom', which can be felt as well as heard. While described as an 'alarm' sound, this noise was used by Mr Blue to settle the chick Matangi.

It is difficult to take such a showy, portly bird seriously — one wonders if it was designed by committee. The plumage, a rich mix of blues and greens, is best appreciated close-up. Like pukeko, takahe have a pure white patch of feathers under the tail, used for sexual display. The plumage is strikingly accessorised by their massive red beak and legs. Visitors, eager for their first sight of a takahe, often mis-identify a distant pukeko. Guides point out that the smaller, lighter pukeko can fly, albeit poorly, while the takahe, over three times heavier at three kilograms, certainly cannot! Takahe chicks don't seem to know this and one fluffy youngster (Mungo) stretched up tall and flapped its stubby wings furiously, jumping up and down in an attempt to get airborne.

There's a delightful photo of Orbell and his companions having a leisurely lunch in the company of tethered takahe on that special day in 1948.[3] Lunch on Tiri today is even better, because the takahe roam free as a bird. But picnics on Hobbs Beach can be a nightmare, with Greg, the most confident takahe, intent on stealing food. Guides mount a 'Greg watch' on summer weekends to protect the boaties from Greg, and vice versa. He's had a flipper thrown at him, and one man — mistaking him for a stroppy pukeko — was barely stopped from braining him with

A few years ago when Dr Geoffrey Orbell was in his nineties (he is still alive), he was taken back by helicopter to the site where he rediscovered the takahe to release some young captive-reared takahe back into the wild.[4]

a plank. Admittedly it is difficult to convince people that Greg is one of the rarest birds in the world, as he patrols the crowded beach. When a woman was sunbathing with a straw hat over her face, Greg marched right across the hat, and he has stolen a plastic bag containing women's underwear while the owner was swimming. In summer 2004, Greg brought his mate and chick Tiri down to join in the fun (see photo page 113).

Takahe are opportunistic feeders rather than pure vegetarians. On Tiri they eat baby quail, and a group is suspected of devouring a clutch of brown teal ducklings near the wharf dam. On the beach, they will catch and eat sandhoppers. Greg once discovered bees drinking from a puddle. The first ones he ate must have stung him because from then on he carefully drowned each bee before swallowing it.

One takahe has snatched a passing fantail on the wing, and Stormy once caught a hawk! When found, he had it pinned down on its back with his powerful red foot and was plucking feathers from its breast. The hawk was minus its lower jaw, and in such shock that it made no effort to defend itself with its talons. Takahe have a claw on their 'elbow' with which to rake their opponents in a fight. Ray Walter has been clawed when holding a bird.

Left: The Lighthouse gang in 2000. Anne Rimmer

Far left: A powerful beak. Alex Mitchell

Below far left: Why Greg is an OSH hazard — Matt Low is the victim. Matt Low

Below left: Takahe chicks have an 'egg tooth' on the end of their beak. Anne Rimmer

The takahe, so nearly extinct, are a metaphor for all the New Zealand birds which are genuinely gone for good, and can never be rediscovered. And they are a powerful reminder of the many other species that hover perilously close to extinction.

They are birds of the open grassland rather than the dense bush, and areas at the southern end of the island have been specially planted for them. With their powerful beak they pluck the grass and eat the fleshy stem at the base of the leaves. Undigested material colours their copious eight-centimetre-long, sausage-shaped droppings green.

The Tiri population of takahe may not have had a spectacular breeding success, but their impact as 'ambassadors for the endangered' has been huge.

~

SEVENTEEN

KOKAKO — THE GIFT OF SONG

From the deepest parts of the forest a kokako calls: soft, sustained notes with a woodwind quality — like a flute or an organ. The listeners stop and hold their breath, willing the unseen bird to continue. It comes again, in a minor key, ineffably haunting. The kokako's song tugs at the heartstrings, distilling in its purity the whole story of the destruction of New Zealand's wildlife.

North Island kokako
Callaeas cinerea wilsoni
Protected; threatened; endemic.

If takahe are the clowns of Tiritiri, kokako are the wairua, the spirits of the forest. One of the most loved birds is the aptly named Te Koha Waiata (TKW), The Gift of Song. This male, raised at Mount Bruce, was released with two others on 10 August 1997 in a public release attended by 200 people. He paired up with a female brought from Mapara in the central North Island named Cloudsley Shovell (after a British Admiral). Four more birds were released on 21 March 1998, and the population on Tiri now stands at about 15 birds.

TKW and Cloudsley, as they are known, have raised most of the kokako chicks on Tiri, granting us remarkable insights into kokako life in the process. It is common to see the devoted pair feeding or bathing together or singing from the same tree, for TKW to land on a branch above someone's head, or to see the caring father shuttling between two teenage offspring, one on each side of the track, unconcerned at the cluster of people observing them.

In 2003 the pair had a second nest, the location of which was very hard to keep secret. (Kokako can raise two clutches a year in different nests.) They built the nest in December, in the crown of a ponga beside the Wattle Track. The hundred or more people who walk that track each day passed directly beneath it. And from the steps above, anyone in the know could eyeball a sitting kokako or, by January, watch the baby being fed. While the adults have circular blue wattles on the cheeks, baby kokako have pink ones. One chick was named Ruby for her red bands and also after Ruby Jones who studied kokako.

The news is not all good, however. The kokako on Tiri may be safe from the mammalian predators, particularly stoats, that are wiping out the mainland populations, but they are attacked by Australasian harriers: chicks disappear soon after hatching. A camera trained on the nest filmed two of TKW and Cloudsley's chicks being eaten in February 2004. This is distressing for the people as well as the parents, as everyone has a strong empathy for these trusting birds.

As well as their haunting song, the birds say their name, 'kokako'. They are noticeably larger than tui and their energetic movements are distinctive, as they bound or run along the ground or spring athletically from branch to branch through the trees. They can glide well on their stubby wings, but are barely able to gain height.

Kokako spend a lot of time on the ground. This bird (TKW) is eating weeds on the Wharf Road.
Peter Craw

Facing page: The male kokako, Te Koha Waiata (The Gift of Song), performing 'archangel', flapping his wings.
Alex Mitchell

Below: Te Koha Waiata, exhibiting his usual curiosity. Alex Mitchell

Right: A fledgling kokako showing the pink baby wattles, the colour just turning to blue.
Matt Low

Below right: Schoolgirls marvel at the location of the now-empty kokako nest on Wattle Track.
Anne Rimmer

A disturbing incident occurred in 2001. The island was rejoicing over the hatching of two female kokako chicks to TKW and Cloudsley, after their first clutch had been predated. DOC officers from the northern conservancy, plus a Maori kaumatua, arrived unexpectedly and removed the nest containing the two 15-day-old chicks. DOC's kokako recovery group's plan was to raise the two females in zoos, pairing them with males from the Puketi Forest.[1] Owing to predation, there are no females left in Puketi, and this genetic line will die out without human intervention.

While the science may be sound, the way it was done was not, and the sense of loss and indignation among the Supporters on Tiri that day was intense. Simon Fordham's editorial in the *Dawn Chorus* was restrained: 'DOC have a responsibility, as they carry out their duties to consult with interested parties. In this case, the relevant iwi were consulted … but we were not.' One bird died in captivity a few months later; the second, Tiri Waiata, remains at Auckland Zoo. Ray and Barbara Walter and many volunteers visit her there.

EIGHTEEN

INTO THE FUTURE

'Tiri was one of the achievements of my time on the Hauraki Gulf Maritime Park Board.
Visited there recently, can't see a thing for trees …' – Tony Kendall

So, what of the future for this fortunate island? The prognosis is excellent: Tiri's open sanctuary concept is an undoubted success, both from the birds' and people's points of view. The challenge now is to improve the quality of visitor experience while coping with the inevitable escalation in visitor numbers. Rob McCallum, DOC's Auckland conservator, says: 'Undoubtedly, the biggest challenge will be in ensuring that Tiritiri is not "loved to death" — the management of visitor numbers will become critical and setting it correctly will provide for some robust debate.'

It is worth noting that the people who designed the Tiri project — Bob Drey, Neil Mitchell and John Craig — planned not for hundreds, but for thousands of visitors per day, and though they are happy and proud of what Tiri has become, they feel it could and should go much further. This does not mean one ferry disgorging 1000 passengers at 10 am and removing them at 3 pm. As John Craig points out, 'the middle of the day is a lousy time to see birds anyway'. Craig also asks why every visitor must receive the same experience: at present, even repeat visitors get the same guided tour. He advocates dawn and dusk tours.

However, Ray and Barbara Walter and the majority of the volunteers who help run the island want little or no increase in visitor numbers, fearing that it would degrade the visitor experience, and increase their workload beyond an acceptable level. Certainly, if the present regime continues, the energy and availability of volunteers will be a limiting factor to growth.

John Craig has strong feelings about the importance of getting people to pay for a conservation experience and at present a visitor who is not guided pays nothing towards the island's upkeep. But Barbara Walter points out that some families already find the boat fare expensive, and since Tiri is an open sanctuary it would be impossible to police any entrance fee.

The Wattle Valley, regenerating since the 1970s, is now densely forested.
Gareth Eyres/Exposure
(courtesy of *North & South*)

'This is a delightful bird, and with its engaging personality it will soon become a firm favourite with the children and adult visitors to the island.'

– Barbara Hughes

North Island tomtit

North Island tomtit, miromiro
Petroica macrocephala
Protected; endemic.

This transfer was facilitated by a Supporter, Barbara Hughes, with Kevin Parker and Tim Lovegrove from ARC providing the scientific support. Richard Griffiths (DOC, Warkworth) had originally suggested that Barbara, a teacher, carry out the task during her Royal Society Teaching Fellowship year.

The documentation process comprised the initial translocation proposal, consultation with seven iwi, a 30-page document to deal with objections that had been raised, and some extensive negotiations for budget and contract time with SOTM committees. A further permit was required when DOC called for disease screening of some of the birds.

Meanwhile, Barbara and her team (which included a research student, Sonja Gerritsen, from Van Hall Instituut, Holland) were visiting the area in the Hunuas where Waytemore Forests Ltd were to be clear-felling exotic pine forest on leased ARC land. They visited the area two to three times a week to 'habituate' the tomtits — getting them used to being fed so that they could be caught more easily. She found that the females were far more cautious than the males, but by

capture day most of the resident birds and their territories were known to Barbara.

On 14 April 2004, four capture teams were in place by 7 am. The tomtits were lured into mist nets, from which they were rapidly extracted, and taken to 'central processing'. Here they were weighed, measured and banded before being put into individual boxes for transportation by car and helicopter to Tiri.

An astounding 23 birds were caught on the first day, with nine more the next day.

Thirteen of the 32 tomtits transferred were female, which is very pleasing.

The tomtits all survived the journey, which included a tense drive through Auckland's rush-hour traffic. They were released into selected bush areas, but many dispersed quite quickly.

She spent several days on the island monitoring the birds after release. A group on a guided walk saw one the day after it had been released, and several other individuals have been sighted since.

It will be interesting to observe any interactions between the tomtits and their relatives, the North Island robins.

Over 20 people helped with the translocation, which was funded by the Supporters, ARC and DOC.

Postscript: When Barbara revisited the Hunuas two months later, she was astounded to see a banded tomtit. 'Mr RG' was back in his original territory. This tiny 10-gram bird, who was transported to Tiri in a closed box, had flown 63 kilometres home over unknown and unseen territory.

The black and white male tomtit brings a mealworm to his mate (photo taken in the Hunuas). Barbara Hughes

As hard as it is to contemplate, the retirement of Ray and Barbara Walter will inevitably bring change. Fortunately everyone has had time to prepare so that the transition can go as smoothly as possible. The Supporters, who fund many of the projects on the island as well as putting in so many volunteer hours, must be consulted when DOC is appointing replacements for these two guardians of Tiri. Ray, while disparaging what he calls 'the cult of personality', thinks that the island should be staffed by two couples plus a single man. Barbara hopes that their replacements will 'nurture people' and have 'the philosophy from the heart'. She feels that 'people, education, birds and weeds' are the key elements for their successors to focus on.

As far as the restoration project is concerned, the hardest work is done, with maintenance plus some 'tweaking' needed in the future. From the visitor's point of view the trees may be at an ideal height right now, with everything happening at eye level. As the trees grow taller some bird activity will rise up out of view.

Some people feel that some of the early plantings need thinning. Ray Walter and John Craig want to go in with chainsaws to cut 'light wells' in the forest every 10 years or so. Others, including Neil Mitchell and Ewen Cameron, want the island left to sort itself out.

'It is a marvellous place and deserves to be celebrated.'
– David Attenborough, 2004

Climate change will bring more extreme weather to Tiri: higher winds, more storms, more drought and extremes of temperature. For both the flora and fauna of Tiri this represents more stress. Perhaps there will be more food in extremely good years, but this will be offset by disasters in times of severe weather. There is nothing we can do to prepare the island for future natural disasters. It must just, literally, weather the storm.

Ray and Barbara Walter.
Gareth Eyres/Exposure
(courtesy of *North & South*)

But what happens if the process of 'sorting' affects an endangered species, as happened when the kakariki population exploded a few years ago? It will be many years until the island's ecosystem is truly in balance, and until then swings of the pendulum could be disastrous. Should we not remain with a hand on the tiller in case a change in direction is needed? As Ray Walter warns, 'Just remember, you are manipulating Mother Nature and sometimes she wins.'

There is unfinished business in the missing microfauna (e.g. reptiles, invertebrates) and microflora (e.g. ferns) and these gaps should be filled. Some researchers complain that DOC's paper trail gets longer rather than shorter. Why did it take so long for

Tiri to get tuatara when over on Little Barrier Island the tuatara population languished in pens because kiore were still present on that sanctuary?

With its predator-free status, Tiri should continue to produce more birds than its small size can accommodate. As such, it is an ideal site to provide birds for other projects. Tiri has already sent saddlebacks to Mokoia and Moturoa Islands, Karori Sanctuary and Mount Bruce; North Island robins to Wenderholm and Great Barrier Island; and whiteheads to the Hunuas. Soon there may be enough stitchbirds to give some away as well.

Nevertheless, Barbara Walter warns that Tiri's needs must come first: there is still a noticeable reduction in saddleback numbers in Wattle Valley since 40 birds went to Karori in 2002.

Tiri's current working plan contains a wish list for future releases. It includes: 'rifleman, giant weta ... flax snails, bats and at least 10 species of lizard. Very few translocations of these have been attempted and those that have occurred have had only limited success.'[1]

Tiri's influence has spread in many ways: many conservation projects now involve the public as a matter of course. People come from other conservation areas to learn how we do it. Unfortunately, in Ray's experience they don't always heed his advice.

While Tiri conservationists have actively sent birds out to go forth and multiply, other species have managed the process without assistance; kakariki and bellbirds have flown over to Whangaparaoa, and both now breed there. The author waits with bated breath for the first bellbird in her Rothesay Bay garden.

People have also gone forth from Tiri: there are scientists spread throughout New Zealand who, having worked on Tiri, use the knowledge gained there to aid conservation elsewhere. Most have a special affection for Tiri, something that can only help the island in the future. International conservationists like David Bellamy and David Attenborough are familiar with Tiri and spread the word internationally. Two Australian and two UK projects have sought advice from Tiri.

'The green revolution is an unstoppable force for good, a revolution which will work because people are not fighting each other, simply getting on with the job.'

– David Bellamy

Something to really sing about: a male stitchbird celebrates life on Tiri.
Peter Craw

Tiri is not a zoo; it is the public that is confined while the birds roam free. Most birds do not suffer from the controlled presence of humans on the island: some, such as takahe, positively thrive on it!

Of major concern is the tardiness of the next island sanctuary, and the next, to come on line. It is many years since John Craig and Neil Mitchell wrote the proposals for Rangitoto, Motutapu, Motuihe and Motuora Islands, but none has yet become the safety valve for Tiri, as Tiri was created to take the pressure off Little Barrier Island. Mainland 'islands' such as Tawharanui and the Waitakeres' Ark in the Park are positive signs, as could be 540-hectare Kaikoura Island, off Great Barrier Island.

The remarkable thing about Tiritiri Matangi is that even during a short day's visit, almost everyone is touched by its magic. This small, unprepossessing island, so close to a metropolis of over one million people, is a place where birds and people live and move through the forest in harmony, where it is almost mandatory to slow down so that even the busiest visitor has time to observe at close range the subtle gradations of colours in a takahe's plumage, to marvel at the fragile delicacy of a robin's legs, or be moved by the haunting beauty of the kokako's song. To see and hear the raucous, jaunty saddleback, so full of vitality on Tiri, and to reflect that this bird had previously been clinging

It is a tradition to wave goodbye from the wharf (cf. page 92). Matt Low

Astronomy

Far from the city lights, the stars on Tiri are gloriously bright and infinitely numerous. In 2001 the Supporters and the Auckland Astronomical Society organised a stargazing trip that sold out well in advance. Even though it was a cloudy night and stargazing was barely possible, the trip was a big adventure for all involved. Anders Hansen must have been asked to look for the first appearance of Halley's Comet (which came in 1910) because in 1907 he wrote to Cheeseman, 'No sign of comet or comets yet.'

to life on one small island, is a sobering reminder of how badly we have degraded New Zealand, our island home. We have fouled our nest in a way no bird would tolerate.

Those who are lucky enough to have a closer association with Tiri, visiting regularly, observing the patterns of the seasons, working there and staying overnight, all refer to it as 'paradise'. The constant music of bird calls is soothing in an almost hypnotic way. One arrives tense, and leaves with a calmer disposition. It is an environment that brings out the best in people.

Much of the credit for the harmony comes from the human guardians. Ray Walter is a remarkable man, modest, hard-working, and devoted to this island that he has lived on and served in such disparate capacities for over 20 years. Ray's abilities and achievements merit a full book of his own. And his wife, Barbara, has incredible energy and efficiency. She is a fount of knowledge about the island and the people who visit, remembering names and details of a visitor she may not have seen for years. On top of all this, she is responsible for much of the bird observation.

Many feel it is the most successful conservation project they have been involved with.

The moon silhouettes
Tiritiri Matangi lighthouse.
Pat Greenfield

*'If we all walked
away tomorrow,
the island would
just carry on.'*

– Ray Walter

NOCTURNE

When the ferry departs, full of tired, happy people, a few smug individuals remain on the wharf, waving goodbye. And as they turn away, the island belongs to them. The afternoon and evening pass quietly with no visitors to deal with, no ferry to catch.

At dusk, the pace in the bunkhouse quickens: researchers prepare hearty meals after a day's work, or before setting off for a night of fieldwork, and people materialise, warmly clad, fitting red cellophane to their torches and asking anxiously for the best places to see kiwi.

Kiwi hunting is one of the great rewards of staying on Tiri, and with over 50 kiwi on the island, there's a good chance of seeing one. The 'old hands' each have a different technique. Ray Walter says to wait till quite late, but others start at nightfall. Some people set out in groups, while others prefer to wander round alone. Faint lights of other hunters can be seen, wavering

around on the hillsides, as everyone disperses to their chosen areas. Simon and Morag Fordham, who have an excellent track record, walk fast, sweeping a strong torch across the undergrowth, looking for the movement of a kiwi ducking as the beam passes it. Others target a likely area, listening for the purposeful tramp of big feet through the leaves, or the snuffle as a kiwi clears dirt from its nostrils.

The first surprise is that, even standing at the base of the lighthouse, one cannot see the wheeling beams, except where they brush the tip of the Norfolk Island pine.

Soon after dark the first kiwi calls, a male, its loud, rising trill repeated 10 or more times. The sound is very directional — the bird's mate has emerged from her own burrow and is already walking towards it — and so are the humans, guessing the sound came from the nursery area. If they are lucky, they will get a close-up view. The kiwi may even approach them, a soft fawn ball with an amazingly long beak. It taps their shoe. There's a pause as the bird analyses the sensation, then it jumps in fright and rushes off. If a kiwi calls from nearby, your ears will ring! And if you stumble over one in the dark, it snaps its beak, a terrifying sound when unexpected.

But other creatures are awake, too: a pukeko screams; seabirds murmur from the rocks below; tuatara are about in the forest; robins occasionally sing at full moon; and from all around comes the soft rasp of weta. Soon there may be bats fluttering overhead as well.

Down at the beach, penguins are coming in for the night and walking up the tracks. Grey-faced petrels at nesting time fly noisily overhead, before landing and shuffling into their burrows. (Helping to band petrels is another reward of a stay on Tiri.)

Stay out for long enough, and a subtle lessening of the darkness, a faint red line on the eastern horizon, and the first sleepy notes of a tui herald the dawn. There's no point in going to bed now. Might as well settle down somewhere comfortable to enjoy the rousing dawn chorus, which welcomes another day on Tiritiri Matangi, the fortunate island.

Appendix A: Birds of Tiritiri Matangi

Eighty-four species of birds have been seen on or close to Tiritiri Matangi.

TRANSLOCATED BIRDS

Brown teal (pateke), *Anas aucklandica chlorotis*

Fernbird (matata), *Bowdleria punctata vealeae*

Little spotted kiwi (kiwi pukupuku), *Apteryx owenii*

North Island kokako, *Callaeas cinerea wilsoni*

North Island robin (toutouwai), *Petroica australis longipes*

North Island saddleback (tieke), *Philesturnus carunculatus rufusater*

Red-crowned parakeet (kakariki), *Cyanoramphus novaezelandiae novaezelandiae*

Stitchbird (hihi), *Notiomystis cincta*

Takahe, *Porphyrio hochstetteri*

Tomtit (miromiro), *Petroica macrocephala*

Whitehead (popokatea), *Mohoua albicilla*

OTHER BIRDS

Arctic skua, *Stercorarius parasiticus*

Australasian gannet (takapu), *Morus serrator*

Australasian harrier (kahu), *Circus approximans*

Australian magpie, *Gymnorhina tibicen*

Barbary dove, *Streptopelia roseogrisea*

Bellbird (korimako), *Anthornis melanura melanura*

Black petrel (taiko), *Procellaria parkinsoni*

Black shag (kawau), *Phalacrocorax carbo novaehollandiae*

Black swan, *Cygnus atratus*

Blackbird, *Turdus merula*

Blue penguin (korora), *Eudyptula minor*

Brown quail, *Synoicus ypsilophorus*

Budgerigar, *Melopsittacus undulatus*

Buller's shearwater, *Puffinus bulleri*

Caspian tern (taranui), *Sterna caspia*

Chaffinch, *Fringilla coelebs*

Common myna, *Acridotheres tristis*

Diving petrel (kuaka), *Pelecanoides urinatrix urinatrix*

Dunnock, *Prunella modularis*

Eastern bar-tailed godwit (kuaka), *Limosa lapponica baueri*

Eastern rosella, *Platycercus eximius*

Feral goose, *Anser anser*

Flesh-footed shearwater (toanui), *Puffinus carneipes*

Fluttering shearwater (pakaha), *Puffinus gavia*

Galah, *Cacatua roseicapilla*

Giant petrel, *Macronectes halli*

Goldfinch, *Carduelis carduelis*

Greenfinch, *Carduelis chloris*

Grey duck (parera), *Anas superciliosa*

Grey warbler (riroriro), *Gerygone igata*

Grey-faced petrel (oi), *Pterodroma macroptera gouldi*

House sparrow, *Passer domesticus*

Kookaburra, *Dacelo novaeguineae novaeguineae*

Little shag (kawaupaka), *Phalacrocorax melanoleucos brevirostris*

Long-tailed cuckoo, *Eudynamys taitensis*

Mallard, *Anas platyrhynchos platyrhynchos*

Morepork (ruru), *Ninox novaeseelandiae novaeseelandiae*

New Zealand dotterel (tuturiwhatu), *Charadrius obscurus*

New Zealand kingfisher (kotare), *Halcyon sancta vagans*

New Zealand pigeon (kereru), *Hemiphaga novaeseelandiae novaeseelandiae*

New Zealand pipit (pihoihoi), *Anthus novaeseelandiae novaeseelandiae*

North Island fantail (piwakawaka), *Rhipidura fuliginosa placabilis*

North Island kaka, *Nestor meridionalis septentrionalis*

North Island weka, *Gallirallus australis greyi*

Paradise shelduck (putangitangi), *Tadorna variegata*

Pheasant, *Phasianus colchicus*

Pied shag (karuhiruhi), *Phalacrocorax varius varius*

Pomatine skua, *Stercorarius pomarinus*

Pukeko, *Porphyrio porphyrio melanotus*

Red-billed gull (tarapunga), *Larus novaehollandiae scopulinus*

Redpoll, *Carduelis flammea*

Reef heron (matuku-moana), *Egretta sacra sacra*

Rock pigeon, *Columba livia*

Shining cuckoo (pipiwharauroa), *Chrysococcyx lucidus lucidus*

Shore plover (tuturuatu), *Thinornis novaeseelandiae*

Silvereye (tauhou), *Zosterops lateralis lateralis*

Skylark, *Alauda arvensis*

Song thrush, *Turdus philomelos*

Southern black-backed gull (karoro), *Larus dominicanus dominicanus*

Spine-tailed swift, *Hirundapus caudacutus caudacutus*

Spotted dove, *Streptopelia chinensis tigrina*

Spotted shag (parekareka), *Stictocarbo punctatus punctatus*

Spotless crake (puweto), *Porzana tabuensis plumbea*

Spur-winged plover, *Vanellus miles novaehollandiae*

Starling, *Sturnus vulgaris*

Sulphur-crested cockatoo, *Cacatua galerita*

Tui, *Prosthemadera novaeseelandiae novaeseelandiae*

Variable oystercatcher (torea), *Haematopus unicolor*

Welcome swallow, *Hirundo tahitica neoxena*

White-faced heron, *Ardea novaehollandiae novaehollandiae*

White-faced storm petrel (takahikare-moana), *Pelagodroma marina maoriana*

White-fronted tern (tara), *Sterna striata*

Yellowhammer, *Emberiza citrinella*

Appendix B: Trees and Plants of Tiritiri Matangi

This list contains the most prominent trees and plants on Tiri.

(*Alectryon excelsus*) (titoki)

(*Alseuosmia banksii*) (toropapa, pere)

(*Astelia banksii*)

(*Beilschmiedia tarairi*) (tairaire)

(*Beilschmiedia tawa*) (tawa)

(*Brachyglottis repanda*) (rangiora)

(*Carmichaelia arborea*) New Zealand broom

(*Ozothamnus leptophyllus*) (tauhinu) cottonwood

(*Clematis paniculata*) (puawhananga) bush clematis

(*Clianthus puniceus*) kaka beak

(*Coprosma areolata*) thin-leaved coprosma

(*Coprosma* aff. *macrocarpa*) (karamu)

(*Coprosma propinqua*) (mingimingi)

(*Coprosma repens*) (taupata)

(*Coprosma rhamnoides*)

(*Coprosma robusta*) (karamu)

(*Cordyline australis*) (ti kouka) cabbage tree

(*Corokia buddleioides*) (korokio taranga)

(*Corynocarpus laevigatus*) (karaka)

(*Cyathodes juniperina*) (mingimingi)

(*Dianella nigra*) (turutu) blueberry

(*Dodonaea viscosa*) (akeake)

(*Dysoxylum spectabile*) (kohekohe)

(*Elaeocarpus dentatus*) (hinau)

(*Elingamita johnsonii*)

(*Entelea arborescens*) (whau) cork tree

(*Euphorbia glauca*)

(*Fuchsia excorticata*) (kotukutuku) tree fuchsia

(*Fuchsia procumbens*) creeping fuchsia

(*Geniostoma ligustrifolium*) (hangehange)

(*Hebe diosmifolia*)

(*Hebe stricta*) (koromiko)

(*Hedycarya arborea*) (porokaiwhiri) pigeonwood

(*Hibiscus diversifolius*)

(*Hibiscus trionum*) annual hibiscus

(*Ipomoea cairica*) NZ morning glory

(*Knightia excelsa*) (rewarewa) NZ honeysuckle

(*Kunzea ericoides*) (kanuka) tea tree

(*Leucopogon fasciculatu*) (mingimingi)

(*Leptospermum scoparium*) (manuka) tea tree

(*Leptospermum scoparium* var. *keatleyi*) pink tea tree

(*Litsea calicaris*) (mangeao)

(*Macropiper excelsum*) (kawakawa) pepper tree

(*Meilcytus novaezelandiae*) coast mahoe

(*Melicope ternata*) (wharangi)

(*Melicytus ramiflorus*) (mahoe) whiteywood

(*Metrosideros excelsa*) (pohutukawa)

(*Muehlenbeckia complexa*) (pohuehue) wire vine

(*Myoporum laetum*) (ngaio)

(*Myrsine australis*) (mapou) red matipo

(*Olearia furfuracea*) (akepiro, tanguru)

(*Parsonsia heterophylla*) (kaihua) NZ jasmine

(*Phormium tenax*) (harakeke) flax

(*Pittosporum crassifolium*) (karo) turpentine tree

(*Pittosporum umbellatum*) (haekaro)

(*Podocarpus totara*) (totara)

(*Pomaderris* aff. *phylicifolia*) (tauhinu)

(*Pomaderris kumerah*) (kumarahou) golden tainui

(*Poutaria costata*) (tawapou)

(*Pseudopanax arboreus*) (puahou) five-finger

(*Pseudopanax lessonii*) (houpara) five-finger

(*Rhabdothamnus solandri*) (taurepo, waiu-atua) NZ gloxinia

(*Rhopalostylis sapida*) (nikau)

(*Ripogonum scandens*) (kareao) supplejack

(*Schefflera digitata*) (pate, patete)

(*Solanum aviculare*) (poroporo)

(*Sophora microphylla*) (kowhai)

(*Streblus heterophyllus*) (turepo) milk tree

(*Streblus smithii*) Smith's milkwood

(*Tecomanthe speciosa*) NZ bignonia

(*Vitex lucens*) (puriri)

Appendix C: Lighthouse Keepers and Signalmen of Tiritiri Matangi, 1865–1984

Names in bold indicate Principal Keepers or Chief Signalmen. From 1865 to 1913 there were only keepers on Tiri. From 1913 to 1925 there were both keepers and signalmen (signalmen are marked with 'AHB'); from 1925 to 1947 only signalmen; and from 1947 to 1984 only lighthouse keepers. Some names were relieving keepers who were on Tiri for only a short time. N.B. Though this list is fuller than any previously published list, it is still incomplete. Not all the dates, nor all the full names are known.

A. Gibson 1865–67
G. Hand 1865–67
Robert Wilson 1866–73
John Wheeler 1874–79
James McKay 1874–85
John Seith 1878–81
A. F. S. Sandager 1881–83
Felix McGahey 1883–86
John Marsh 1885–90
Robert H. Seighton 1886–89
John Jess 1890–94
Norman Simpson 1890–98
Henry Jacobson 1894–99
T. J. Cox 1898–1900
Alexander Connell 1898–1902
Charles Moeller 1900–02
C. Broughton 1901–02
Peter W. Grayfell 1902–05
Horace A. Wakefield 1902–06
Alexander Duncan 1904–07
Anders Hansen 1906–09
Albert V. Pearce 1907–10
J. F. Raynor 1910–12
W. Creamer 1910–12

James Lyon 1911–13
P. J. Voyle 1913–16
C. N. Trainer 1914–15
T. R. Turner 1916–18
W. K. Cleverly 1916–18
Chris Gow 1916–20
Arnold 1919–21
James Lyon (AHB) 1920–25
I. Owen Lord (AHB) 1921–c.1925
Joshua Stuart Roberts c.1918–24
R. H. Neal 1922–25
McLeod 1923
R. S. Wilson 1925–26
Alfred King (AHB) 1928–36
James Lyon (AHB) 1927–35
Alf Roberts (AHB) 1927–35
William Childs Davies (AHB) 1928–39
George Ramsay (AHB) 1936–39
Henry A. Dunnet (AHB) 1938–39
H. J. Petty (AHB) 1939
Charles Webster (AHB) 1940
McTaggart (AHB) 1940–42
Goodale (AHB) 1942–45
Alfred King (AHB) 1945–47
Bill Ford (AHB) 1945–47
George Chamberlain (AHB) 1945–47
Coulson (AHB) 1947
Rasman 1947
Galvin 1948
Blake 1949
McLean 1949
MacGuiness 1949–50
G. R. Gilbert 1949–50
C. Bowles 1949–50
C. Olsen 1949–52
E. Don Meads 1949–53
Forbes 1950

Bisset 1951
B. Cranston 1951–53
Robertson 1952
Henderson 1953–54
Tom A. Clark 1953–54
A. Olsen 1954
Robertson 1954
T. Rour 1954
T. R. (Bob) Welsh 1954–58
Leif Ericsson c.1955?
Stan H. Rhodes 1955–56
R. S. Johnson 1957–58
Ray Mander 1959–60
Trevor W. Scott 1959–61
P. L. Taylor 1960
R. R. Trainer 1960–62
Poole 1962
Alan Wright 1962
Wallace 1963
Charles H. Mallowes 1963–65
George Holmes 1965
Peter L. Taylor 1965–67
Mike P. Pilone 1965–67
Trevor W. Scott 1967–70
Roger Fowler c.1968
Lee Challis 1967–70
Frank Roe 1970–74
Frank Williams c.1971
Tom A. Clark 1974–79
Ray Walter 1980–84

Sources: interviews; books written by keepers; relatives; Wellington Maritime Museum; NZ National Maritime Museum; Ray Walter; Annette Brown; Pat Greenfield; Wynne Spring-Rice.

Appendix D: Chairs of the Supporters of Tiritiri Matangi Inc.

Jim Battersby 1989–92

Trevor Sampson 1992

Dell Hood 1992–96

Mel Galbraith 1996–99

Peter Lee 1999–2002

Carl Hayson 2002–04

Simon Fordham 2004–

Appendix E: Major Sponsors of Tiritiri Matangi

123 Internet Ltd

3M

Adhesif Print Ltd

Adventure Cruising Co. Ltd

Auckland Meat Processors

Auckland Savings Bank

Bank of New Zealand

Blackmores Ltd

Bob Haldane Ltd

BP Solar (Australia Ltd)

British Council

Central Auckland Forest and Bird Protection Society

Chelsea Sugar

Coast Concrete Construction

Dilmah

Dow Agrosciences

DuPont New Zealand Ltd

ENZA

Fields Pond (USA)

Fullers Group Ltd

Galloway Spi Asia Pacific Ltd

Glenfield Lions

Gulf Harbour Ferries

Helitranz

Hibiscus Coast Service Clubs

Hibiscus Coast Zonta Club

Lanier New Zealand Ltd

LJ Fisher Charitable Trust

Lyndale Nurseries

Maurice Paykel Charitable Trust

Moller Yamaha Ltd

New Zealand Glass Environment Fund

New Zealand Lottery Grants Board

New Zealand Wiremakers

North Shore Royal Forest and Bird Protection Society

Norwich Union Life Insurance (NZ) Ltd

Nufarm

Rennie Dowsett Architects

Safetread

Sierra Fertilisers

Sir John Logan Campbell Residuary Estate

State Insurance Ltd

Supporters of Tiritiri Matangi Inc.

The Conservation Alliance (Australia)

Tindall Foundation

University of Auckland

Westad Signs

Wilkinson Smith Contractors

World Wide Fund for Nature Supporters Group Auckland

Yates

Appendix F: Key People

(SOTM = Supporters of Tiritiri Matangi Inc., HGMPB = Hauraki Gulf Maritime Park Board)

ARNOTT, Frank
Board secretary of HGMPB 1977–85

BATTERSBY, Jim
Founder of Supporters of Tiritiri Matangi Inc. (SOTM) 1988

BOLLONS, John Peter, 1862–1929
Captain of *Tutanekai* and *Hinemoa*
lighthouse supply and service

CHEESEMAN, Frederick, 1845–1923
Curator and botanist, Auckland Museum

COCKAYNE, Leonard, 1855–1934
Botanist (visited Tiri pre-1905, 1905 and 1923 etc.)

COLE, Michael
Landscape architect for HGMPB
(on Tiri 1982–83)

CRAIG, John
University of Auckland ecologist
(on Tiri from 1974 onward)
Proposed Open Sanctuary concept

CREAMER, William Eric H., 1907–c.1973
Son of a keeper (on Tiri 1910–12, aged c.3–5)
Wrote *The Tall White Tower* (unpublished)

DAVIS, Sir Ernest, d. 1964
Businessman, philanthropist,
former mayor of Auckland
Donated Davis Marine Light to
Tiri lighthouse 1965

DUNNING, Shaun
Tiri volunteer and DOC employee
(on Tiri 1994–2001)

ELL, Gordon
Forest and Bird, Conservation Board

ESLER, Alan
DSIR botanist, early plant survey, 1971

FORDHAM, Simon and Morag
Long-time supporters
Simon is current SOTM chairman

GALBRAITH, Mel and Sonya
Tiri volunteers since 1983
Mel is former SOTM chairman

GEDDES, Eric
Forest and Bird, Tiri volunteer since early 1980s
Built saddleback boxes

GILBERT, G. R.
Keeper c.1956
Wrote *Love in a Lighthouse*

HANSEN, Anders, immigrated 1875, d. 1939
Keeper on Tiri 1906–9
Conservationist

HOBBS, Everard John (Johnny), d. 1947.
Held Tiri farm lease from 1902

HOBBS, John Norman (Jack), 1907–92
Farming involvement 1907–71
Daughters Daisy (Burrell) and Margaret, known as Peggy

HOLDAWAY, Jim
HGMPB, chairman of Parks Board, later, Tree Council, Conservation Board etc.

HOLLAND, Mark
Supporter, built the Wattle and Kawerau Tracks with his friends

HOOD, Dell
Former SOTM chair

KAY, Malcolm C., d. 2002
Naval Reserve (on Tiri, September 1939–40)
Known as 'Ginger' or 'Jenner'
Married Nancy Davies, AHB signalman's daughter, 1942

KAY, Nancy (née DAVIES)
Father, Owen DAVIES, keeper

KING, Alfred
AHB signalman (on Tiri, 1928–36 and 1945–47)
Wife, Bessie; children, in order, Pat (Meyer), Alf, Reg, Dora (Walthew), David, Betty (Roper)

LADD, Fred, 1908–89
Flew amphibian plane for
Tourist Air Travel Ltd

MITCHELL, Neil
University of Auckland botanist
(on Tiri from 1978 onwards)
Proposed Open Sanctuary concept

O'BRIEN, Darcy
Commissioner of Crown Lands, HGMPB, WWF

RAE, Lola, née LORD, 1907–
Lived on Tiri 1921–22 as a teenager
Father, Owen Lord, AHB signalman during the 1920s.

SCOTT, Trevor
Lighthouse keeper 1950s and 1960s

SILVESTER, Ralph
Forest and Bird, plantsman, volunteer in early 1980s

SPRING-RICE, Dr Wynne
Archaeologist for HGMP

TAYLOR, Peter
Lighthouse keeper 1960s

TURBOTT, Graham
HGMPB, museum director, ornithologist, author

USSHER, Graham
Herpetologist (helped on Tiri August 1990–present)

VEITCH, Dick
Wildlife Service officer, then DOC
Organised first bird transfers

VELVIN, Jan
SOTM and plant expert

WALTER, Barbara
Present DOC conservation officer on Tiri (on Tiri since 1980s)

WALTER, Lynda
Daughter of Ray and Val Walter
(on Tiri as a teenager, 1980–82)

WALTER, Ray
Last lighthouse keeper, till 1984,
then ran the Tiri project
Present DOC conservation officer on Tiri

WEST, Carol
First botany thesis on Tiri, 1980

Bibliography

BOOKS

Auckland Harbourmaster's Letter Book 1851, New Zealand Historic Places Trust, Auckland.

Bercusson, L., *The Hauraki Gulf*, Macmillan/Shoal Bay Press, Auckland, 1999.

Burstall, S. W., and Sale, E. V., *Great Trees of New Zealand*, Reed: New Zealand Forest Service, 1984.

Cameron, E., Hayward, B. and Murdoch, G., *A Field Guide to Auckland*, Godwit, Auckland, 1997.

Carson, Rachel, *Silent Spring*, Houghton Mifflin, Boston, 1962 [1994].

Cheeseman, T. F., *Manual of the New Zealand Flora*, Government Printer, Wellington, 1906 [1925].

Clark, T. A., *The Sea Is My Neighbour*, Whitcombe and Tombs, Christchurch, 1963.

Durrell, G. M., *Two in the Bush*, HarperCollins, London, 1966.

Ell, G., *Wild Islands, Exploring the Islands of the Hauraki Gulf*, Bush Press, Auckland, 1982.

Falla, R. A., Sibson, R. B. and Turbott, E. G., *Collins Field Guide to the Birds of New Zealand*, HarperCollins, Auckland, 1993.

Gilbert, G. R., *Love in a Lighthouse*, Pegasus Press, Christchurch, 1956.

Harding, P. ed., *Lonely Planet Guide to New Zealand*, 11th edition, Lonely Planet, Melbourne, 2002.

Hauraki Gulf Maritime Park, Hauraki Gulf Maritime Park Board, 1986.

Heather, B. and Robertson, H., *Field Guide to the Birds of New Zealand*, Viking, Auckland, 1996.

Ingram, C. W. N. and Wheatley, P. O., *New Zealand Shipwrecks*, Hodder Moa Beckett, Auckland, 1990.

Johnson, D., *Triumph: the Ship that Hit the Lighthouse*, Dunmore Press, Palmerston North, 1941.

Lee, W. G. and Jamieson, I. G., *The Takahe: Fifty Years of Conservation Management and Research*, University of Otago Press, Dunedin, 2001.

Maddox, S. and White, D., *Islands of the Gulf*, Collins, Auckland, 1966.

Moon, L. and G., *The Singing Island: the Story of Tiritiri Matangi*, Godwit, Auckland, 1998.

Morris, R. and Smith, H., *Saving New Zealand's Endangered Birds*, Random House, Auckland, 1995.

Pollock, Mabel, *The Children from the Lighthouse*, Pollock Books, Auckland, 1993.

Pope, D. and J., *Mobil New Zealand Travel Guide, North Island*, Reed Methuen, Auckland, 1984.

Reed, A. W., *The Reed Dictionary of New Zealand Place Names*, Reed Books, Auckland, 2002.

Ross, J. O'C., *The Lighthouses of New Zealand*, Dunmore Press, Palmerston North, 1975.

Salmond, A., *Between Worlds: Early Exchanges Between Maori and Europeans, 1773–1815*, Viking, Auckland, 1997.

Taylor, P. L., *As Darker Grows the Night*, Hodder and Stoughton, Auckland, 1975.

ARTICLES

Arcus, P. 'Profile: Peter Arcus', in *Weiti Boating Club Newsletter*, Whangaparaoa, 2002.

Brebner R., 'Tree-mendous Effort on Tiritiri', in unknown newspaper, 12 August 1989.

Cameron, E. K. and West, C. J., 'Notes on the Flora of Tiritiri Matangi Island, Hauraki Gulf', in *Tane* 31, 1985–86, pages 121–123.

Carey, Peta, 'Finding Richard Henry', in *New Zealand Listener*, Auckland, 3 August 2002.

Craig, J., Mitchell, N., Walter, B., Walter R., Galbraith, M. and Chalmers, G., 'Involving People in the Restoration of a Degraded Island: Tiritiri Matangi Island', in *Nature Conservation 4: the Role of Networks*, eds., Saunders, D. A., Craig, J. L. and Mattiske, E. M., Surrey Beatty & Sons, 1995.

Davidson, Janet, 'Maori Prehistory: the State of the Art', in *Journal of the Polynesian Society* 92, 3, 1980, pages 291–307.

'Duke Hails Work on Island Havens', in *New Zealand Herald*, 2 March 1992.

Esler, A. E., 'Botanical Features of Tiritiri Matangi Island, Hauraki Gulf, New Zealand', in *New Zealand Journal of Botany* 16, 1978, pages 207–226.

Frewen, T., 'Putting Roots Down on Tiri', in *Gulf News*, 18 May 1984.

Gill, B., 'The Secretive Singer', in *Forest & Bird* 310, November 2003.

Galbraith, M. P. and Hayson, C. R., 'Tiritiri Matangi Island, New Zealand: public participation in species translocation of the North Island robins to an open sanctuary', in *Reintroduction Biology of Australian and New Zealand Fauna*, ed. Serena, M., Surrey Beatty & Sons, Chipping Norton, 1994, pages 149–154.

Gladwell, Jack, 'Mains Power to Tiri Tiri Island', in *Ministry of Works Gazette*, vol. 4, no. 3, September 1967.

Grzelewski, D., 'Kakapo: Bird on the Brink', in *NZ Geographic* 56, 2002, pages 20–42.

Hansford, D., 'Coming Home to Roost', in *Forest & Bird* 310, November 2003.

'Island Sanctuary', in *New Zealand Woman's Weekly*, 21 April 1986.

'Lighthouses of New Zealand', in *Evening Post*, Wellington 1931, ASB January 1988, page 48 (APL).

'News from the Hauraki Gulf', in *Friends of the Hauraki Gulf Maritime Park*, no. 3, December 1990.

Orsman, B., 'Call to Reopen Island Lighthouse', in *New Zealand Herald*, 12 January 2004.

'Poison Blitz on Gulf Island Rats', in *New Zealand Herald*, 11 June 2004.

Rimmer, A., 'Forest Mimic Copies Call of the Kokako', in *Forest & Bird* 307, February 2003.

'Safeguarding the Port', in *Auckland Star*, 21 February 1913.

Sibson, R. B., 'Bird Notes from Tiritiri Island 1945–1946', in *Tara*, September 1991 (reprinted in B11).

Stamp, R. K. and Brunton, R. H., 'An Investigation into the Impacts of Mites and Nest Box Design on the Reproductive Success of the North Island Saddleback', in *New Zealand Journal of Zoology* 29, 2002, pages 285–292.

'This Housekeeping is for the Birds', in *DuPont* magazine, January–February 1992.

'Tiritiri Matangi Island', in *Friends of the Hauraki Gulf Maritime Park*, no. 1, June 1990.

Vayda, Andrew P., 'Maoris and Muskets in New Zealand: Disruption of a War System', in *Political Science Quarterly* LXXXV, 4, 1970, pages 560–584.

Veitch, D., 'Little Barrier, Looking Back and Adding Up', in *HGMP Newsletter*, no. 31, January 1981.

Walter, B., 'Report from Tiritiri', in *Friends of the Hauraki Gulf Maritime Park*, no. 1, June 1990.

Wynne, M., 'By Tiri's Light She Ran Aground', in *Auckland Star*, 10 August 1962.

MANUSCRIPTS AND CORRESPONDENCE

Cheeseman, T. F., 1908, Letters from A. Hansen, held at the Auckland War Memorial Museum Library, Auckland.

Cheeseman, T. F., 1908, Letters from A. Hansen, incomplete species list (Tiritiri Matangi Island), held at the Auckland War Memorial Museum Library, Auckland.

Cockayne, L., 1905, Notebook 21, Leonard Cockayne manuscript collection (MS 74), Auckland War Memorial Museum Library, Auckland.

Creamer, W. E., 'The Tall White Tower', unpublished manuscript, National Library of New Zealand, Wellington, c.1965.

Habgood M., 'Behavioural Interactions between Copper and Moko Skinks', MSc thesis, University of Auckland, 2003.

Hagan (née Petty), Agnes, memoir written for Wynne Spring-Rice, c.1985

Hansen A., Letters to Cheeseman, 1906–09, Auckland War Memorial Museum Library, Auckland.

Roper (née King), Betty, memoir written for Wynne Spring-Rice, c.1985.

Walthew (née King), Dora, memoir written for Wynne Spring-Rice, c.1985.

Walthew (née King), Dora, memoir, c.1985.

Walthew (née King), Dora, memoir, 26 February 1994.

REPORTS

Cole, M., 1983, *Progress Report to the HGMPB*, held in Tiri Archives, Tiritiri Matangi Island.

Esler, A. E., *Report to Hauraki Gulf Maritime Park Board*, Auckland, 1971.

Hawley, J. G., *Tiritiri Matangi Working Plan*, New Zealand Department of Conservation, Auckland Conservancy, Auckland, 1997.

Historic Places Trust Report, October 1988.

Spring-Rice, W., *Final Archaeological Report, Tiritiri Matangi Island*, Anthropology Department, University of Auckland, 1981.

Tiritiri Matangi Island Working Plan, Department of Lands and Survey for the Hauraki Gulf Maritime Park Board, Auckland, 1982.

Treadwell Associates, *Conservation Plan for the Tiritiri Matangi Island Lighthouse Complex*, prepared for the Department of Conservation, Auckland, 1997.

Wright A., 'Report to the Wildlife Service', 1962.

LEGISLATION

Historic Places Act 1980

OTHER

AJHR H 15, 1908, page 5.

Dawn Chorus, Bulletin of the Supporters of Tiritiri Matangi Inc.

'Guide Weekly', Supporters of Tiritiri Matangi Inc.

'Guiding Manual', Supporters of Tiritiri Matangi Inc.

Hauraki Gulf Maritime Park Newsletter, Hauraki Gulf Maritime Park Board.

NZ Geographic 55, January–February 2002, (cover photograph).

Rodney and Waitemata Times, 2 August 1988.

The Postman, annual magazine of the Correspondence School, December 1929.

Tiritiri Matangi file, Department of Conservation.

Tiritiri Matangi logbook of ship sightings for 1907–15.

University News, vol .7 (2), University of Auckland, Auckland, April 1977.

WEBSITES

ARC: www.arc.govt.nz

Correspondence School: www.correspondence.school.nz

Department of Conservation: www.doc.govt.nz

Fullers Group Limited: www.fullers.co.nz

King's College Old Collegians' Association: www.kcoca.com

Kiwi Wildlife Tours: www.kiwi-wildlife.co.nz

Maritime Safety Authority: www.msa.govt.nz

New Zealand Underwater Association: www.NZunderwater.org.nz

New Zealand National Library, Wellington: www.tapuhi.natlib.govt.nz

New Zealand National Maritime Museum: www.nzmaritime.org.nz

Supporters of Tiritiri Matangi Island Inc.: www.tiritirimatangi.org.nz

The Royal Forest and Bird Protection Society of New Zealand: www.forest-bird.org.nz

Warbirds (Alex Mitchell's Tiri photography): www.warbirdsovernewzealand.com

WWF (formerly known as the World Wildlife Fund): www.panda.org or www.wwf.com

Notes

INTRODUCTION

1 OE = 'overseas experience' — the year or more that young New Zealanders traditionally spend abroad.

ONE: NOW — AND THEN

1 E. Cameron, B. Hayward and G. Murdoch, *A Field Guide to Auckland*, Godwit, Auckland, 1997.

2 J. Morton (ed.), *A Natural History of Auckland,* Auckland Regional Council, Auckland, 1993.

3 *ibid.*

TWO: A TIME OF PLENTY — THE MAORI

1 R. K. Nichol, 'Excavation at the Sunde Site on Motutapu', Archaeology Department, University of Auckland. *HGMP Newsletter*, issue 32, April 1981.

2 H. Leach, *1000 Years of Gardening in New Zealand*, Reed, Wellington, 1984.

3 L. Bercusson, *The Hauraki Gulf*, Macmillan/Shoal Bay Press, Auckland, 1999.

4 H. Leach, *1000 Years of Gardening in New Zealand*.

5 *ibid.*

6 A. Salmond, *Between Worlds: Early Exchanges Between Maori and Europeans, 1773–1815*, Viking, Auckland, 1987.

7 J. Davidson, 'Maori Prehistory: the State of the Art', *Journal of the Polynesian Society* 92, 3, 1980.

8 S. P. Smith, *Maori Wars of the 19th Century*, Whitcombe and Tombs, Wellington, 1910, cited in *Tiritiri Matangi Island Working Plan*, Department of Lands and Survey, for the Hauraki Gulf Maritime Park Board, Auckland, 1982.

9 A. W. Reed, *The Reed Dictionary of New Zealand Place Names*, Reed Books, Auckland, 2002.

10 D. and J. Pope, *Mobil New Zealand Travel Guide, North Island*, Reed Methuen, Auckland, 1984.

11 R. H. Locker, *Jade River*, Friends of Mahurangi Inc., Warkworth, 2001.

12 *Hauraki Gulf Maritime Park,* Hauraki Gulf Maritime Park Board, Auckland, 1986.

Other information in this chapter was sourced from: B51.

THREE: THE PASTORAL CENTURY

1 W. E. Creamer, 'The Tall White Tower', unpublished manuscript, National Library of New Zealand, Wellington, c.1965.

2 E. J. Hobbs, diary, 1898.

3 E. J. Hobbs, diary, 1899.

4 E. J. Hobbs, diary, 1905.

5 W. E. Creamer, 'The Tall White Tower'.

6 C. W. N. Ingram and P. O. Wheatley, *New Zealand Shipwrecks*, Hodder Moa Beckett, Auckland, 1990.

7 J. N. Hobbs, interview by Pat Greenfield, 1991.

8 bach = a rough holiday cottage. This was the earlier 'men's house', the shearers' quarters.

FOUR: ILLUMINATION

1 Candlepower = a standard spermaceti candle used as a unit of illuminating power. = 1869 Roscoe Elem. Chem. (*Compact Oxford English Dictionary*).

2 E. Cameron, B. Hayward and G. Murdoch, *A Field Guide to Auckland*, Godwit, Auckland, 1997.

3 J. O'C. Ross, *The Lighthouses of New Zealand*, Dunmore Press, Palmerston North, 1975.

4 T. A. Clark, *The Sea Is My Neighbour*, Whitcombe and Tombs, Christchurch, 1963.

5 The keepers wore special blue glasses called 'lamp-trimmer's glims'. Ray Walter still has a pair. Ray Walter, conversation with author, 16 August 2003.

6 As well as Tiri, these were Taiaroa Head, Mana Island, Godley Head and Dog Island.

7 The concrete base appears to be inscribed W. Ward / I. Blair / D.Hatril / M. Cole / 4.10.83.

8 Mabel Pollock, *The Children from the Lighthouse*, Pollock Books, Auckland, 1993.

9 www.msa.govt.nz/Safety/Lighthouses/history.htm accessed 28 May 2004.

10 W.E. Creamer, 'The Tall White Tower', unpublished manuscript, National Library of New Zealand, Wellington, c.1965.

11 Similarly, in the Hauraki Gulf today, the beacon on Maria, in the Noises group, is sectored white/red to indicate the D'Urville Rocks.

12 Reported by Tiri Gow, Jack Hobbs and Russell Miell.

13 G. R. Gilbert, *Love in a Lighthouse*, Pegasus Press, Christchurch, 1956.

14 www.nzmaritime.co.nz/hin1.htm accessed 28 May 2004.

15 *Ibid.*

16 W. E Creamer, 'The Tall White Tower'.

17 G. R. Gilbert, *Love in a Lighthouse*.

18 Dora Walthew, interview by Wynne Spring-Rice, c.1985.

19 *ibid.*

20 Russell Miell, interview by Pat Greenfield, 27 May 1992.

21 Charles Brazier, interview by Pat Greenfield, 27 May 1992.

22 D. Walthew, 'If Only', *Historical Review Bay of Plenty Journal of History*, vol. 34, no. 1, May 1986.

23 G. R. Gilbert, *Love in a Lighthouse*.

24 Dora Walthew, interview by Pat Greenfield, 26 February 1994.

25 E. Cameron, B. Hayward and G. Murdoch, *A Field Guide to Auckland*.

26 David Johnson, *Triumph: the Ship that Hit the Lighthouse*, Dunmore Press, Palmerston North, 1941.

27 W. E. Creamer, 'The Tall White Tower'.

28 *New Zealander*, 4 February 1865.

29 *New Zealand Herald*, 8 August 1913.

30 Tiritiri Matangi log book of ship sightings for 1907–15.

31 Dora Walthew, interview by Pat Greenfield, 26 February 1994.

32 Dora Walthew, née King, memoir, c.1985.

33 AJHR 1908, H 15 (page 5).

34 Dora Walthew, née King, memoir, c.1985.

35 G. R. Gilbert, *Love in a Lighthouse*.

36 P. L. Taylor, *As Darker Grows the Night*, Hodder and Stoughton, Auckland, 1975; Peter Rhodes, conversation with author, 9 November 2003.

37 Dora Walthew, née King, memoir, c.1985.

38 *ibid.*

39 'Lighthouses of New Zealand', *Evening Post*, Wellington, 1931, ASB January 1988 (page 48) (APL).

40 King sisters, interview by author, 18 September 2003.

41 W. E Creamer, 'The Tall White Tower'.

42 Dora Walthew, née King, memoir, c.1985.

43 G. R. Gilbert, *Love in a Lighthouse*.

44 A. Hansen, letters to Cheeseman 1906–9, Auckland War Memorial Museum Library.

45 Dora Walthew, memoir, 26 February 1994.

46 D. Walthew, 'If Only'.

47 G. R. Gilbert, *Love in a Lighthouse*.

48 Nancy Davies, 'Correspondence School', *The Postman*, December 1929.

49 G. R. Gilbert, *Love in a Lighthouse*.

50 T. A. Clark, *The Sea Is My Neighbour*.

51 Heather Cochrane, née Mander, letter to author, 2003.

52 Lola Rae, née Lord (at age 97), interview by author, 9 February 2004.

53 D. Walthew, 'If Only'.

54 King sisters, interview by author, 18 September 2003.

55 D. Walthew, 'If Only'.

Other information in this chapter was sourced from: B48.

FIVE: ON ACTIVE SERVICE

1 Malcolm Kay, interview by Pat Greenfield, 27 April 1992.

2 *ibid.*

3 *ibid.*

4 *ibid.*

5 *ibid.*

6 Letter to the naval secretary, Wellington, 12 March 1943 (in Tiri Archives).

7 Willoughby 'Bluey' Wheldale, interview by Pat Greenfield, c.1991.

SIX: MODERNISATION

1 The cowshed was demolished in 2004 ('Guide Weekly', 21–27 Jan 2004).

2 Betty Roper, née King, memoir, written for Wynne Spring-Rice, c.1985.

3 P. L. Taylor, *As Darker Grows the Night*, Hodder and Stoughton, Auckland, 1975.

4 Jack Hobbs, interview by Pat Greenfield, 8 July 1991.

5 Russell Miell, interview by Pat Greenfield, 27 May 1992.

6 P. L. Taylor, *As Darker Grows the Night*.

7 S. Maddock and D. White, *Islands of the Gulf*, Collins, Auckland, 1966.

8 Written on *New Zealand Herald*, 21 December 1966 (in Tiri Archives).

9 P. L. Taylor, *As Darker Grows the Night*.

10 ' ...Final chapter now complete', Auckland Public Library, ASB S8/9 newspaper cutting, 8 September 1965.

11 Ray Walter, talk to Tiri guides, 26 November 2001.

12 Frank Arnott, email to author, 15 May 2003.

13 Russell Miell, interview by Pat Greenfield, 27 May 1992.

14 *ibid.*

Other information in this chapter was sourced from: B24.

SEVEN: THE DAWN CHORUS

1 R. A. Falla, R. B. Sibson and E. G. Turbott, *Collins Field Guide to the Birds of New Zealand*, HarperCollins, Auckland, 1993.

2 B. Heather and H. Robertson, *Field Guide to the Birds of New Zealand*, Viking, Auckland, 1996.

3 E. Cameron, B. Hayward and G. Murdoch, *A Field Guide to Auckland*, Godwit, Auckland, 1997.

4 B. Heather and H. Robertson, *Field Guide to the Birds of New Zealand*.

5 A. Hansen, letters to Cheeseman 1906–9, Auckland War Memorial Museum Library.

Other information in this chapter was sourced from: B1, B2, B6, B11, B12, B14, B16, B19, B23, B27, B28, B31, B32, B36, B38, B40, B43, B44, B45, B46, B47, B48, B49, B50, B54, B55.

EIGHT: GERMINATION

1 DSIR = Department of Scientific and Industrial Research (a now-defunct government department).

2 A.E Esler, 'Report to Hauraki Gulf Maritime Park Board', 1971.

3 Dick Veitch, interview by author, 11 February 2003.

4 'Guiding Manual', Supporters of Tiritiri Matangi Inc.

5 John Craig, interview by author, 30 January 2003.

6 Ray also brought a half-built boat, the *Burgess Island*, which stood up at the lighthouse while he finished it off. See photo of Tiri lighthouse and boat in *Lighthouses of New Zealand*.

7 *Tiritiri Matangi Island Working Plan*, Department of Lands and Survey, for the Hauraki Gulf Maritime Park Board, Auckland, 1982

8 Minutes of committee meeting, 30 July 1983 (in Tiri Archives).

NINE: THE FLORA

1 The term 'reafforestation' is the one used in the reports of the time. Many of today's familiar words such as ecology and eco-sourcing were not yet in common use.

2 L. Cockayne, Notebook 21, AR Ms 74 (page 9), Auckland War Memorial Museum Library.

3 A. Hansen, letters to Cheeseman 1906–9, Auckland War Memorial Museum Library.

4 The trees form the 'ears' of Tiri's sleeping hippo shape.

5   *Tiritiri Matangi Island Working Plan*, Department of Lands and Survey, for the Hauraki Gulf Maritime Park Board, Auckland, 1982.

Other information in this chapter was sourced from: B42.

TEN: THE SPADE BRIGADE

1   M.Cole, 'Progress Report to the HGMP Board', 26 July 1983 (in Tiri Archives).

2   Neil Mitchell, interview by author, 28 February 2003.

3   T. Frewen, 'Putting Roots Down on Tiri', *Gulf News*, 18 May 1984.

4   R. Brebner, 'Tree-mendous Effort on Tiritiri', unknown newspaper, 12 August 1989.

5   Swanndris = bright-coloured plaid wool shirts.

6   Gordon Ell: former member of the Conservation Board, former national president of the Royal Forest and Bird Protection Society of New Zealand, and current editor of *Forest & Bird* magazine.

7   *Rodney and Waitemata Times*, 2 August 1998.

Other information in this chapter was sourced from: B18, B27, B37, B43, B47, B50, B52.

ELEVEN: SUPPORT

1   Jim Battersby, interview by author, 3 December 2002.

2   *ibid.*

3   Barbara says that when the takahe later known as Greg arrived on Tiri 'he had a boring name like Mr Green or something'.

4   Tiri takahe release leaflet, 1991.

5   DOC's cautious approach continues today. Kakariki have been introduced to Somes Island, a predator-free sanctuary in the centre of Wellington Harbour. But the first release was of male birds only, 'to investigate their effect on the vegetation'.

6   A scheme for school leavers designed to help them get a feel for conservation.

Other information in this chapter was sourced from: B1, B3, B5, B6, B7, B9, B10, B14, B16, B23, B27, B30, B36, B37, B47, B50, B53.

TWELVE: THE UNWANTED

1   In the 1980s an attempt was made to teach the endangered saddleback to cope with rats. Birds were transferred to Kapiti Island (which then had rats) in the hope that some of them might learn to nest above the ground. Two hundred and fifty saddleback were transferred over a number of years in this experiment.

2   It is important to note that Tiri has the North Island robin, not the very rare Chatham Islands black robin of which 'Old Blue', the female that saved the species, is the most famous example.

3   At the Karori Wildlife Sanctuary, young mice have shown they can get through the supposedly impervious fence. Further bird transfers are on hold for the moment. Source: D. Hansford, 'Coming Home to Roost', *Forest & Bird*, November 2003.

4   Trevor Scott, letter to Pat Greenfield, 1995.

5   Mike Lee, email to author, 28 March 2003.

Other information in this chapter was sourced from: B15, B38, B41, B44, B45, B48.

THIRTEEN: THE NON-BIRDS

1   www.doc.govt.nz/Conservation/001-Plants-and-Animals/001-Native Animals/Invertebrates/Giant Weta.asp

2   wetapunga = God of ugly things.

Other information in this chapter was sourced from: B13, B17, B21, B34, B35, B47, B50, B55.

FOURTEEN: THE PARALLEL UNIVERSE

1   A 'grad student' conducts a body of research towards a higher degree, under the supervision of a faculty member. A Master of Science (MSc) takes two to three years and a Doctor of Philosophy (PhD) three years or more; both usually require a thesis. Research papers are often published subsequently.

Other information in this chapter was sourced from: B18, B21, B22, B44, B52.

FIFTEEN: FRUITION

1   Chris Gulley, 'Tiritiri Matangi', *Wilderness Magazine*, website: www.nzkayak.co.nz/articles.htm

2   Slang for types of transport.

3   NativeZ is Sonya Galbraith's company. Soft-toy versions of native birds are sold in the Tiri shop.

Other information in this chapter was sourced from: B13, B16, B19, B21, B23, B24, B26, B28, B31, B32, B34, B36, B37, B38, B39, B41, B43, B44, B45, B46, B47, B48, B51, B52, B53, B54, B55.

SIXTEEN: TAKAHE — AMBASSADORS FOR THE ENDANGERED

1   W. Lee and I. Jamieson, *The Takahe: Fifty Years of Conservation Management and Research*, University of Otago Press, Dunedin, 2001.

2   Shirley Nieuwland, conversation with author, January 2004.

3   W. Lee and I. Jamieson, *The Takahe: Fifty Years of Conservation Management and Research*.

4   *ibid.*

Other information in this chapter was sourced from: B8, B38, B50.

SEVENTEEN: KOKAKO — THE GIFT OF SONG

1   Puketi Forest is in Northland, inland from the Bay of Islands.

Other information in this chapter was sourced from: B33, B48.

EIGHTEEN: INTO THE FUTURE

1   Carl Hayson, 'From the Chair', B55.

Other information in this chapter was sourced from: B17, B22, B25, B28, B41, B45.

Index